DECODING THE MYSTERY
OF EXCELLENCE

DECODING THE MYSTERY OF EXCELLENCE

Lessons from the experiences of Shechem

RICHARD AMOAYE

Published in Sydney, Australia
by Dominion Publishers

First published 2016
This edition published 2021

© 2021 Richard Owusu Amoaye

All rights reserved. No part of this publication may be reproduced, stored in a retrieval system, or transmitted in any form or by any means—for example, electronic, mechanical, photocopy, recording—without the prior written permission of the publisher. The only exception is brief quotations in printed reviews.

For licensing/copyright information, for additional copies or for use in specialised settings contact: info@richardamoayeministries.com

Emphasis in Scripture highlighted in bold is the author's.

Unless otherwise identified, Scripture quotations are from the New King James Version. Copyright ©1982. Used by permission of Thomas Nelson, Inc. All rights reserved.

Scripture quotations labeled NIV are from the Holy Bible, New International Version®. NIV®. Copyright © 1973, 1978, 1984 by Biblica, Inc.™ Used by permission of Zondervan. All rights reserved worldwide. www.zondervan.com

Scripture quotations labeled AMP are from the Amplified® Bible, Copyright © 1954, 1958, 1962, 1964, 1965, 1987 by The Lockman Foundation. Used by permission.

 A catalogue record for this book is available from the National Library of Australia

ISBN 978 0 6481259 4 5 (pbk)

Cover designed by Vanguard House
Typeset by Blue Wren Books
Printed by Lighthouse Print Group

CONTENTS

Dedication — vii
Acknowledgements — ix
Prelude — xi
Foreword — 1
Preface — 3
Introduction — 7

1. **Shechem: The Breeding Ground for Excellence** — 15
   The Shechem Experience — 16
   Shechem: The Place to Encounter God — 22
   The Medium of Excellence: Our Divine Destiny — 27

2. **Excellence in the Making: Joseph's Story** — 31
   Welcome Your Test of Responsibility — 31
   Be a Reliable Child — 34
   Encounter the Certain Man — 36
   Favour Attracts Your Destiny Helpers — 41
   Upgrade Your Favour — 44
   Care for the Distressed — 47
   Gallop into Your Destiny — 49

3. **Shorten Your Walk to Destiny: Lessons from Abraham** — 53
   - Don't Stray from Your Bethel — 54
   - Watch Out for Your Destiny Hijackers — 56
   - Negotiate Your Way Around Transit Posts — 59
   - Dealing with the Lot Kind — 61
   - Wait for Your Isaac — 63

4. **Stay Awake on Your Path to Destiny: Isaac's Predicament** — 69
   - The Price of Carnality — 70
   - Having Dominion Over Veils — 76
   - Explore Your Shechem to the Fullest — 81

5. **A Supplanting Spirit Will Prolong Your Walk to Destiny: Jacob's Adventure** — 85
   - Twisting the Arm of God — 86
   - A Reverse Walk — 89
   - Crossing the Jordan is Not Enough — 93

6. **Overcoming the Self: Joseph's Brothers** — 103
   - Control Your Lustful Desires — 104
   - Deal with Your Temper — 109
   - Remain Spiritually Alert at All Times — 112

7. **The Mystery Behind Joseph's Bones** — 117
   - Carry My Bones with You — 118
   - Divine Keys to Excellence — 120
   - The Different Lifestyles in Perspective — 123

Conclusion — 125

About the Author — 127

DEDICATION

This book is lovingly dedicated to my biological parents. Dad, Odeefuo Owusu Amoaye II, your role as traditional ruler of your community, sixty-five years of dedicated leadership, has been a positive influence in my life. Your lifestyle and counsel have inspired me by way of reinforcing my resolve to strive for excellence in all that I do. You taught me that the cornerstone of leadership is service in truthfulness.

Dad, thank you for your generosity which ensured that I did not become a burden on the churches that hosted me in the early days when I was an itinerant minister. The revelations in this book would have been impossible to share without your willingness to be used by God to be an exemplary father. May the good Lord continue to bless you with long life and may your service in His kingdom be a memorial in His presence.

Mum, my beloved Oheneyere Yaa Serwaa (Auntie May), thank you for your prayers and continuous belief in me, particularly in those challenging formative years before I came to the saving grace, because they ultimately led me to Christ Jesus. Mum, this book is a token of my profound love and appreciation of you. Your tears and your prayers were not in vain. I love you so much.

ACKNOWLEDGEMENTS

This book was made possible by the God factor. I want to thank God for His guidance and for revelations granted me throughout. I want to thank Him for the wonderful people who enabled me to bring this project to fruition.

I want to thank my wife, Patrice, whose love, dedication, and many helpful insights enabled me to write this book. Patrice, you are a continuous source of encouragement. You are truly God's gift to me.

Eric L. Kanyoke, my spiritual son, thank you for your dedication and commitment to the structural and editorial work on this project. I deeply appreciate your labour.

To my daughters in the Lord Amanda Mayengehama, Romina Blankson, Eugenia Marembo, Elaine Batsilas and Eva Batsilas for the final edit, thank you for supporting Eric in this project.

To all the workers at God's Power Ministries, thank you for your passionate commitment and dedication to the call of God upon my life. You make my work easy and you bring joy to my heart.

PRELUDE

Excellence, Wisdom, Power, Favour and Grace are among some of the most commonly used words by Christians. These words form part of the language and principles of God. Yet, for many believers, these words and the language of God remains a mystery.

The modern era has afforded us access to a lot of information, worldviews, and voices. Unfortunately, in the process, many biblical meanings and terms have been conflated with the 'modern man's' philosophies. The result has been a blurring of lines between what seems good and what is truly godly. In addition, the potency of God's word and the effect it can have in the life of a believer continues to be compromised!

The *Decoding Series* seeks to address the ongoing tensions between the worldly and godly perspective many believers wrestle with daily. In each volume, Prophet Richard explores and unpacks the biblical meanings and mysteries surrounding these keywords and principles. *Decoding the Mystery of Excellence* is the first book in this exciting volume of inspired reads!

FOREWORD

One key ingredient that influences people into glorious destiny is the Force of Excellence. It is embedded in the very nature of Divinity. You do not need to search far to discover that God is a God of excellence. Creation and its operation clearly support this claim. If that is so, then it stands to reason that the people of God should walk and operate in the same vein.

It is excellence that separates the achiever from the underachiever. Indeed, you may be loaded with talent, ability, goodwill and noble intentions, but if you lack excellence in your life and dealings, you will languish in the crowded bottom life. Like Daniel, excellence will distinguish you in this fiercely competitive world.

In this book, Rev. Amoaye will take you on a deliberate journey to help you unravel the mysteries that often surround this all important subject. You will discover that excellence is neither an event nor a fad. You will learn that it is a lifestyle that is enforced by a strong ethic.

This book will carry you along and teach you that, wherever you may find yourself, whether it is in ministry, family, the corporate world or any leadership position, you will need the spirit of excellence to succeed. It will speak in your absence and promote you over more 'qualified' people. I must warn you that it may not be an easy journey because excellence is always resisted by the mediocre. You will have to be steadfast as you walk in the way of superior service.

Let this book be like a textbook of life. Read it with openness of heart and purpose. Endeavour to put the discoveries you will make into practice. You will begin to walk in higher levels of achievement as you journey towards your glorious destiny.

Rev. Dr. Frank Ofosu-Appiah,
Senior Pastor and Founder,
All Nations Church, Loganville, GA

PREFACE

If the title of this book caught your attention, chances are you have already given serious thought to what excellence is and the kind of destiny considered to be dynamic. To avoid getting lost in the semantics, I am going to explain exactly what I mean by 'decoding the mystery of excellence'. The use of the word 'excellence' refers to the brightness of life described in Isaiah 60:3. I am talking about the kind of brightness that attracts the attention of the world's kings and nobles. It is a life that always seeks godly responsibility, a life of valuable impact on the lives of others, a life devoted to the common good, and a life that leaves an inspiring legacy to future generations. This life is characterised by selflessness, responsiveness to the needs of people, and concern for the well-being of others.

If you were hoping for a book of steps to help you achieve an excellent destiny, a fast track to a successful life, or even a specific place where a fulfilled destiny can be realised, I'm sorry to disappoint as this is not that book. If you are looking for the kind of excellence that is long lasting and trans-generational, then the truths revealed in this book will be of tremendous help to you.

Conventional wisdom tends to over emphasise the effectiveness of self-ability. We've been told that the way to achieve an excellent destiny is by committing to working hard and smart. The God factor is left out of the equation. On the other hand, religious traditions particularly Christianity have over emphasised the role of God's grace in achieving excellence. As humans we aspire to acquire excellent destinies, however, many of us fail to achieve this. A crucial element is missing from both these viewpoints. We may value hard work, smartness, or dedication to religious beliefs, but due to deficient traits in personality, temperament, and appetite, which get in the way, we fall short of that standard. This is due mainly to the fact that often we do not spend adequate time purging ourselves of the things that limit our ability to be responsible. We tend to avoid environments where purging can be induced.

In the following pages we are going to explore this dilemma together. We will see that in spite of pressure and the temptation to do otherwise, we are able to fulfill the dream of achieving excellence in our destiny. Along the way I hope to convince you that the 'mystery of excellence' can lead you to the inspirational discovery of the truth regarding the meaning of responsibility. This is often missed in the rush to realising an excellent destiny. For over two decades, in my role as minister of the gospel, and in my service in the capacity of associate pastor, itinerant minister and senior pastor, I have preached to many. I have served and counseled people from all walks of life including theologians, pastors, and church elders, whose personal stories have inspired me to write this book. I have concluded that the crucial truths that underpin the spirit of excellence have not been taught adequately. This book, therefore, contains truth that is intended to fully equip every single person aspiring to a fulfilled destiny.

I offer *Decoding the Mystery of Excellence* to you in the hope that you will learn from the example of Joseph. It is my

Preface

prayer that as you read this book, and as you meditate on its revelations, they will affirm and instill in you a mindset that will lead you to true and lasting success.

INTRODUCTION

A common misconception that has arisen among many within the body of Christ in this end time, is the belief that excellence comes by default once one becomes a child of God. Many Christians believe excellence to be a gift of the Holy Spirit whilst others consider it to be a fruit of the Spirit or even a component of the heritage of the believer that is embodied automatically at the point of rebirth through grace.

As believers we have a tendency to forget that grace actually contains an element of 'godly responsibility' that triggers its functionality. It was the Apostle Paul who encouraged his spiritual son Timothy, and by extension encourages us, to be strong in the grace we have in Christ Jesus in 2 Timothy 2:1. Even though the Apostle Paul has gone to be with the Lord, his words still relate to believers in this end time. The Apostle makes clear that the trigger that activates the grace of Christ Jesus is knowledge of His person. The grace of Jesus is accessed by those who sincerely and eagerly pursue a deeper relationship with Him, who desire to know Him intimately. This was what the Apostle meant in his admonition of Timothy when he instructed him to pursue the keys to the fullness of this grace by

Decoding the Mystery of Excellence

> '... study(ing) to shew thyself approved unto God, a workman that needeth not to be ashamed, rightly dividing the word of truth'.
>
> 2 TIMOTHY 2:15

The Bible states, in Daniel 5:12 that excellence is actually a spirit, 'In as much as an excellent spirit ... (was) found in this Daniel ...' and in Daniel 6:3, 'Then this Daniel distinguished himself above the governors and satraps, because an excellent spirit was in him...' Excellence is imparted by the Holy Spirit and is attracted to godly character. Not all environments are ideal for this impartation to take place. Consider people such as Joseph and Daniel in the Bible whose names have become synonymous with affliction on the one hand, and on the other, by way of enduring trials and overcoming difficulties, the lives of these men ultimately resulted in excellence. We also see this illustrated in the book of John where the Apostle tells of a situation where Jesus had to go through Samaria on his way to Galilee,

> 'Therefore, when the Lord knew that the Pharisees had heard that Jesus made and baptised more disciples than [John the Baptist] (though Jesus Himself did not baptise, but His disciples), He left Judea and departed again to Galilee. But **He needed to go through Samaria**.'
>
> JOHN 4:1-4

It is obvious in this scripture that Jesus was doing something good for the spiritually poor in the region of Judea. Guess who opposed his missionary work there! Not John the Baptist and his followers, as might have been expected, but the Pharisees. The scripture tells us that due to this opposition, Jesus went to his home region of Galilee to do a similar work, but on his way, He decided to stop over in Samaria. In this narrative, a paradox presents itself. A paradox that is inherent in

Introduction

Jesus's decision to stopover, in order to rest in Samaria, of all places. We know that in Jesus's day Jews resented Samaritans because they were considered unclean as we see in John 4:9. The question that springs to mind, therefore, is why would Jesus choose Samaria as a transit point on his way to Galilee given that this was so? Why didn't Jesus choose a holier city like Bethel, for example, which would have been within the vicinity of Samaria and as such easily accessible?

> **The seed of excellence is responsibility.**

I believe that in mentioning that Jesus had to go through Samaria on his way to Galilee, the Apostle John was not simply talking about a geographic convenience. He was revealing Jesus's intent to practically demonstrate how one activates the spirit of excellence. He wanted to teach us the simple principle of responsibility. That is, how to share the gift He freely gave us with others. In other words, before you can enjoy a fulfilled destiny, you must go through a wilderness experience. You need to pass through your individual 'Shechem', translated as godly responsibility, in order to excel in this life. Wilderness experiences develop our capability to shoulder the burdens of others. I believe this was the reason Jesus chose to go through Shechem which was in Samaria rather than go via the easier route to Galilee which would have been through Decapolis east of the Jordan River.

This narrative resonates with many believers. As the Pharisees opposed Jesus, likewise for us it is when we intensify our pursuit of God that we encounter the toughest battles in life. There is a simple reason for this. The enemy knows that in that pivotal decisive moment the trajectory of our life shifts and we are on the way to fulfilling destiny. Yet this is where many of us miss the mark and allow the enemy to steal what we have been building. As believers, the battles we encounter in life are an attestation that we are on the right path to an excellent destiny. The enemy throws trials our way whenever he realises he is losing his grip on us. It is during moments of trial that we need to keep our spiritual lives burning with the fire of the Holy Spirit, thus maintaining laser focus.

During wilderness seasons we need to ascend the mountain of prayer and fasting with unwavering faith in our God. It was King Solomon who said, *"there is a time for everything"*. As believers, we need to be sensitive to times and seasons. This was the mystery Jesus was unveiling to his disciples in the book of John, when He chose to detour through the city of Shechem. This is the mystery He wants you and I as believers in these last days to grasp.

The Apostle Paul also made an interesting statement in the Book of Galatians where he demonstrated how his own wilderness experience in Arabia served as the catalyst for the embodiment of the outstanding spirit of excellence that was so evident in his life,

> *But when it pleased God, who separated me from my mother's womb and called me through His grace, to reveal His Son in me, that I might preach Him among the Gentiles,* ***I did not immediately confer with flesh and blood****, nor did I go up to Jerusalem to those who were Apostles before me; but* ***I went to Arabia****, and returned again to Damascus.*
>
> GALATIANS 1:15-17 (NKJV)

Introduction

There is a striking similarity between Jesus and the Apostle Paul in this scripture. In the latter part, the Apostle Paul talks about the purpose of his call. Notice how his destiny was predicated on the divine agenda of Christ and not on his personal interests. Notice also that as a direct result of his challenging encounter on the road to Damascus, he realised his life was no longer about himself but about how much of Christ's burden, that is, the Kingdom of God, he could carry.

He adds that without delay he went to Arabia, which is a wilderness and a desert. As I pause to ponder on the spirit that persuaded Paul to take such an adventure at that time, I also think about the obvious physical challenges that are typically associated with inhabiting a desert or a wilderness for any length of time.

> **We need the serenity of the wilderness to keep us focused on Christ Jesus.**

Furthermore, it was the same Holy Spirit that led Christ Jesus to the wilderness after He was baptised by John the Baptist, who persuaded Paul to go to the Arabian wilderness.

It is interesting to note how the challenging circumstances of wilderness environments have the ability to equip and prepare us for use by our Lord and master Jesus Christ as vessels of honour.

In the book of Daniel, the Queen of Babylon was privy to a strange problem tormenting King Belteshazzar. The King was perplexed as he had no idea about how to best deal with a difficult situation that had been revealed to him in a dream. It was in the middle of this crisis that the great works of Daniel were remembered:

> *Inasmuch as an **excellent spirit**, knowledge, understanding, interpreting dreams, solving riddles, and explaining enigmas were found in this Daniel, whom the king named Belteshazzar, now **let Daniel be called, and he will give the interpretation.**"*
>
> DANIEL 5:12 (NKJV)

Here the queen reveals her inherent understanding of the connection between Daniel's spirit of excellence and his possession of extraordinary knowledge and understanding which had been demonstrated in his ability to interpret dreams, and his ability to solve difficult problems.

In Daniel 1:4 we read that upon capturing Judah, King Nebuchadnezzar had decided to take for himself some young men, along with treasures from the Temple of God which was in Jerusalem, back to Babylon. The criteria King Nebuchadnezzar used when choosing the Hebrew men was that they had to be highly educated, and they had to possess a superior aptitude for learning Babylonian systems and way of life. It doesn't surprise, therefore, that Daniel was the only one among the Hebrew captives in Babylon who brought to God's remembrance His prophetic word delivered by Prophet Jeremiah in Jeremiah 29:10 concerning his people. Obviously, he had witnessed the captivity of the children of Israel in Babylon going beyond the appointed time but hadn't yet experienced the fulfilment of the entire prophecy. It took Daniel's diligence, discipline, knowledge, and wisdom (Daniel 1:16–17) to recognise this season and to stand in the gap for his people through prayer (Daniel 9:2–3). This is what godly responsibility is about! Daniel must have attained these values by virtue of time spent in the

Introduction

wilderness of captivity in Babylon. Let's have a closer look at the declaration he made:

> *In the first year of [the reign of King Darius] I, Daniel, understood by the books the number of years specified by the word of the LORD through Jeremiah the prophet, that He would accomplish seventy years in the desolations of Jerusalem. Then I set my face towards the Lord God to make a request by prayer and supplications, with fasting, sackcloth, and ashes.*
>
> DANIEL 9:2-3 (NKJV)

It takes a wilderness experience to render one capable of acquiring the knowledge needed to stand on the word of God and to make decrees and supplications for the liberation of people in bondage. This kind of knowledge does not come to one automatically when one becomes a child of God. We see here how spiritual and studious Daniel actually was.

It takes grace to know the hand of God, but it takes sacrifice to know the person of God.

True knowledge of who God is comes at a cost. It comes with an inconvenience, it comes by way of sacrifice. The kind of sacrifice I'm talking about here is the continual diligent application of oneself to the study of God's Word, His Logos.

In the book of Joshua, we read how God entreated Joshua to meditate on His word day and night so that Joshua could make his way prosperous (Joshua 1:8). Acquiring the true revelation of who God is doesn't come to us by default. It only comes to us when we place demands on it through study and meditation on His Word, The Logos. This process is activated when we shut our door to the world and open ourselves to His Spirit. Shechem, the wilderness, is the laboratory where the ideal environment is created for God to operate in us.

I therefore want to invite you to join me on this journey as I uncover the mysteries surrounding Shechem. On this journey, we will see how various biblical characters navigate the wilderness experience, we will see how they approach this season and how they emerge from it. Once we understand God's rationale for allowing wilderness encounters to be a rite of passage, we can become sufficiently prepared to encounter our own. This then allows Him to lead us unhindered onto the route of His choosing as He leads us into a life of excellence.

1

SHECHEM: THE BREEDING GROUND FOR EXCELLENCE

The word *Shechem* has various meanings in the Bible. It is the name of the ancient Israeli town of Shechem, Nablus for example, and it is also used in scripture to refer to certain people like the son of Hamor the king of the Canaanites. However, the spiritual significance of Shechem goes beyond personality and geography.

In this chapter, we will unveil the unique mysteries surrounding the word *Shechem*, with the aim of understanding vital revelations and principles relating to its meaning in scripture. We will look at historical accounts relating to three interrelated subjects. The first being the Shechem experience, the second, the spirit of excellence, and the third, divine destiny.

It was not by accident that biblical heroes such as Abraham, Isaac, Jacob, Joseph, Moses, Joshua, and even

Jesus Christ himself had respective experiences in Shechem and in the neighbouring towns within Canaan.

In order to have a clear understanding of Shechem in its historical and spiritual context, we must look at the meaning of the word Shechem from the Hebrew mindset.

THE SHECHEM EXPERIENCE

The name *Shechem* in Hebrew means *'shoulder'* or *'responsibility'*.

In the book of Isaiah, the Prophet Isaiah gave a prophecy concerning the coming of Our Saviour Jesus Christ:

> *For unto us a Child is born, Unto us a Son is given; And the government will be upon **His shoulder**. And His name will be called Wonderful, Counselor, Mighty God, Everlasting Father, Prince of Peace.*
>
> ISAIAH 9:6 (NKJV)

In this text, the prophet uses the word *shoulder*. He was giving a synopsis of the manner in which the Kingdom of God was to be delivered to us by Jesus Christ. The prophet also highlights the burden or responsibility that was to be associated with this Kingdom.

In a different submission, the prophet Samuel also used a similar word when he conferred the Kingship of Israel on Saul, the son of Kish the Benjamite. The Bible states that not only was Saul more handsome than all the other children of Israel at that time, but also that,

> *'... from his shoulders upward he was taller than any of the people'.*
>
> 1SAMUEL 9:2 (NKJV)

Besides being good looking, Saul was the most responsible in all of Israel at this particular time. That is, there was no one among his contemporaries who was more sufficiently able to carry the burdens of God's people.

The fact that Kish decided to send his son Saul, assisted by servants, to search for his lost donkeys, is ample evidence that Saul's leadership capability was unquestionable. Kish could have sent his servants on this search mission, especially given the level of uncertainty that was associated with the task. The fact that he tasked his son Saul to lead the mission shows the level of confidence he had in Saul. I believe that Saul would have accomplished similar tasks earlier in his life, with excellence, in order to have gained this level of credibility and the trust of his father.

In my own experience, in a ministry that spans two decades, I have witnessed many believers within the body of Christ craving leadership roles in churches and other secular arenas without having experienced mandatory trials and challenges that must precede these appointments as preparation for the adequate fulfillment of the requirements of purpose. Simply put, there are many people in these roles who have not adequately developed strong enough shoulders to bear their own burdens, let alone the burdens of others. The mere fact that someone may have a skill in a particular field of endeavour does not mean that they are adequately equipped for leadership.

The acquisition of leadership ability depends more on character development than on skill alone. Great leadership requires both qualities to function effectively in tandem. The most effective character development experience is that of persistent triumphing over adversarial circumstances. What do I mean by adversity? It could be accepting a lower-level job, which might be unappealing but is a job which actually contains the necessary adversarial components a person must overcome, resulting in the further development of character.

It is only in experiencing the rudiments of lower-level tasks that one's spiritual character and capacity is developed, rendering one able to shoulder more significant and 'noble' responsibility. Such were the steps that David took prior to confronting and defeating Goliath as we see in 1 Samuel 17:34–37. Here, however, the fact that it was Saul who was commissioned to lead the search party that wandered through the lands of Ephraim, Shalisha, Shaalim, Benjamin, and Zuph in search of his father's lost donkeys, shouldn't surprise at all. It was in fulfilling this task that he encountered the Prophet Samuel who led him into his royal destiny.

The second mark of Saul's capacity for responsibility is inherent in his response to the advice given him by the servant who accompanied him on this challenging mission:

> "Look now, there is in this city a man of God, and he is an honorable man; all that he says surely comes to pass. So **let us go there**; perhaps he can show us the way that we should go." Then Saul said to his servant, "But look, if we go, **what shall we bring the man?**"
>
> 1 SAMUEL 9:6–7 (NKJV)

Not only did Saul's response indicate his inclination and strong desire to know the counsel of God regarding their situation, but it also demonstrated that he was a man with a strong passion for God and an in-depth understanding of sacrificing to Him.

The third and perhaps the most important mark of Saul's sense of responsibility has to do with how he responded to his first challenge as leader of God's people. He had demonstrated the traits of godly responsibility at the familial level, but it appears that these traits were not yet visible to the general public even after he was anointed King, as the following scripture suggests,

> *And Saul also went home to Gibeah; and valiant men went with him, whose hearts God had touched. But some rebels said, "**How can this man save us?**" So they despised him, and brought him no presents but he held his peace.*
>
> 1SAMUEL 10:26–27 (NKJV)

Here we see a man who had demonstrated traits of godly responsibility within his family but who hadn't yet received full public acceptance. Some of his subjects even doubted his ability to lead them. It is certain that although Saul had these traits inside him, they were not publicly visible. The people needed to see ample demonstration of those traits in order to put their faith in him as their leader. He needed an opportunity to show what he was capable of. No wonder when the opportunity presented itself he rose to the occasion:

> *So the messengers came to Gibeah of Saul and told the news in the hearing of the people. And all the people lifted up their voices and wept. Now there was Saul, coming behind the herd from the field; and Saul said, "What troubles the people, that they weep?" And they told him the words of the men of Jabesh. Then **the Spirit of God came upon Saul** when he heard this news, and **his anger was greatly aroused.***
>
> 1 SAMUEL 11:4–11 (NKJV)

Here the narrative begins with a wicked King called Nahash who was intent on troubling God's people in Jabesh. When offered the opportunity to become his servant, Saul declined. The only reason he refused this offer was because he knew that the king had plans to inflict wickedness on God's children. Thank God that for every wicked intention from the enemy's camp there is always a Saul filled with the Holy Spirit to decimate the enemy. I like Saul's response to the troubling news coming from the camp of the wicked King.

First, and most significant, we learn that the people of Jabesh were not heathens. They had a covenant with God and so their cry for liberty from this wicked King was heard by God. However, the solution to their crisis was in the hand of a man called Saul. This man was given this ability and privilege because he was responsible. A call to destiny is a call to responsibility. The more responsible we become the more we can carve out a destiny of excellence for ourselves.

Second, notice what happened when the message about the trouble of the people of Jabesh eventually reached Saul. The scripture says the spirit of God came heavily upon him and made him angry. It was the fact that the solution to this crisis was within Saul, that he needed a witness within himself to release the solution. The anger was the witness that quickened Saul into action. People of God, there is nothing wrong with becoming angry if the reason for your anger is not self-serving and self-centered but rather serves the purpose of executing heaven's agenda. That is, the defence of God's interests.

Third, it is important for us to understand that Saul underwent preparation before the spirit of God came upon him. The scripture says that Saul was returning home from ploughing the field with his six oxen when he heard the news. It is important to identify the kinds of things we need to accomplish in order to be used by the Holy Spirit. It is obvious he had gone to the field (wilderness), to prepare the ground (his heart), to be used by God. In the New Testament dispensation where the Holy Spirit abides in us permanently as believers in Christ Jesus, there are still some preparatory works we must do if we want to operate fully in the supernatural. We must be full of faith and the Holy Spirit as the early church believers like Stephen were (Acts 6:8).

Fourth, even though he could have fought King Nahash and his army single-handedly, given the strength and might of his army, Saul chose to send a message to all the people mobilising support. I like the coding of his message,

> 'Whoever does not go out with **Saul and Samuel** to battle so it shall be done to his oxen.'
>
> 1 SAMUEL 11:7 (NKJV)

Notice he mentions Samuel's name, which represents the presence of God here. That is, to win any battle in life, we need all three vital components in order to be victorious: God, ourselves, and other people. Our battles in life become easier when we constitute the right team.

Finally, by performing due diligence, Saul was able to deliver God's people from the wicked plans of Nahash the Ammonite King. The single amazing thing that qualifies Saul as a man who had a great sense of godly responsibility is captured in the following scripture where,

> 'The people said to Samuel, "Who is he who said, 'Shall Saul reign over us?' **bring the men, that we may put them to death."** But Saul said, "**Not a man shall be put to death this day, for today the LORD has accomplished salvation in Israel.**"'
>
> 1 SAMUEL 11: 12-13 (NKJV)

The best way to silence your enemies is to commit to learning the lessons of godly responsibility.

Godly responsibility was the thing that verified Saul. Notice his response to the people after the victory. We read that whilst the people were calling for blood, he was calling for restraint. Responsible people are not blood thirsty. They don't concentrate on their self-interests but the interests of God. The people were trying to arouse Saul's ego by attributing the credit for the victory to him, but he knew it was God's doing, so he gave the credit to whom it was due. True leaders are not egotistical.

SHECHEM: THE PLACE TO ENCOUNTER GOD

The book of Genesis gives an account of God's creation and the beginning of the human race. It then documents man's fall after heeding the voice of Satan. Following this catastrophic fall, God needed to reconcile man to Himself. To execute His agenda, He chose a particular family to demonstrate His love for mankind. He chose the family of Abraham. Abraham was also named Israel, and by extension the gentile world, through faith in Christ Jesus (Galatians 3:29).

There is one striking similarity in God's encounter with the first three generations of the first family of believers; that is, Abraham, Isaac, and Jacob who are the three great

Shechem

patriarchs of our faith. The similarity is that God's voice to these three great men was most active when they were within the vicinity of *Shechem*. There must have been something that attracted this unique presence of God.

> ## Shechem is the spot where God's voice is most active.

Abraham was called by God to leave his extended family and move to a new. A land that God would show him (Genesis 12:1). At this stage, the details were not made clear to Abraham in that he did not know where exactly God wanted him to go. It was in the middle of this expedition that the specific destination God had in mind became clear to Abraham (Genesis 12:6–7). In the natural realm, this wouldn't have made any sense to Abraham. Yet, he took the step of faith and then the destination God had in mind became evident,

> *Abram passed through the land to the place of Shechem, as far as the terebinth tree of Moreh. And the Canaanites were then in the land.* **Then the Lord appeared to Abram and said, "To your descendants I will give this land."** *And there he built an altar to the Lord, who had appeared to him.*
>
> GENESIS 12:6–7 (NKJV)

Some biblical commentators argue that the first time Abraham heard God's instruction to relocate he was only twenty-five years of age. However, he did not actually respond to this instruction until he turned seventy-five. This means he wasted fifty precious years of his life. I wonder what would have prevented him from acting swiftly upon hearing God's word. I imagine that he would have been walking in accordance with the dictates of his present circumstances and not by faith in God's guidance into his ordained destiny. What a tragedy! I have seen many Christians do the same thing even in these last days. Abraham's destiny could have been aborted midway if he had not been blessed with the grace of long life. Very often when God talks to us He doesn't show us the entire picture until we take the first step of faith.

After Abraham took the initial step of faith, not only did God confirm the location He had had in mind for Abraham at the outset, that is, *Shechem,* as pointed out in Genesis 12:6–7, He also appeared to Abraham in person and spoke to him. When we respond to the voice of God, He then increasingly reveals Himself on a personal level. This scripture goes further to add that Abraham being so impressed by God, went even further by building altars to honour Him within the vicinity of *Shechem* at Bethel. It was therefore surprising to see Abraham vacate this location after such a great manifestation of God's presence. How could one possibly trade Bethel, the House of God, for Egypt which was a pagan land because of famine?

Furthermore, when we look at the life of Isaac, biblical accounts state that his birth and early life, up until the death of his father Abraham, was within the Kadesh region of Beersheba the area of Gerar according to Genesis 25:11. However, we are informed in Genesis 26:1, that there was a severe famine in the days of Isaac, so severe that he had to consult Abimelech the King of the people of Philistine in Gerar. While the Bible is silent about the specific purpose of this consultation, Genesis 26:2 implies that the likely reason for the meeting was to figure a way out of the difficult economic situation Isaac and his people found themselves in at the time. It was in this season of uncertainty that God decided to appear. He revealed to Isaac the way out of the trouble,

> *Then the Lord appeared to him and said: "Do not go down to Egypt;* **live in the land of which I shall tell you. Dwell in this land, and I will be with you and bless you;** *for to you and your descendants I give all these lands, and I will perform the oath which I swore to Abraham your father.*
>
> GENESIS 26:2-3 (NKJV)

In this scripture, there is established the fact that God willed the *promise lands* to Isaac and his descendants through an oath He swore to Abraham. However, the condition attached to this promise was simple, it would only be so '... *if Isaac would dwell in a spot God was to show him called Gerar. Indeed, Isaac dwelled in this place.*' (Genesis 26:6). These are the principles God was teaching Isaac. First, don't try to obtain a solution to the problem from men of strength and authority. Second, rest in this spot and rely only on me. A condition which is also evident in the book of Mathew where Jesus says, "*Come to me, all you who labor and are heavy laden, and I will give you rest*". We all know the positive outcome of Isaac's affirmative response to God's instruction (Genesis 26:12-15).

When we look at the life of Jacob, prior to his encounter with the angel of the Lord, we see that the land God instructed his father Isaac to stay and sow in during the famine was Canaan. The land that he was born in. It was this land that Jacob's destiny was therefore connected to. However, because Jacob subverted his brother Esau's birthright, he had to flee from the location of his destiny. I believe that this specific location was the place that he was ordained to reign with the least effort. The place God had instructed his grandfather Abraham to move away from (Genesis 12:1-4) was the very place Jacob sought refuge in. That is, Haran. Haran was also the place his grandfather Abraham did not want his father Isaac to choose a wife from (Genesis 24:4-8).

It is the Apostle John who presents a narrative in the book of John that I find relates closely to the mystery of Shechem. The Apostle conveys the understanding that Jesus was on his way to Galilee to continue His good works but needed to go through Samaria for some reason, as we see in John 4:1-5,

> *Therefore, when the Lord knew that the Pharisees had heard that Jesus made and baptised more disciples than John (though Jesus Himself did not baptise, but His disciples), He left Judea and departed again to Galilee. But* **He needed to go through Samaria. So He came to a city of Samaria** *which is called Sychar [***Shechem***] near the plot of ground that Jacob gave to his son Joseph.*

It was not a coincidence that Jesus decided to pass through Shechem; and even if we assume that the choice of Shechem was coincidental, we cannot say with certainty that the spot in the city of Shechem where He chose to stay, that is, the plot of land which Jacob gave to Joseph, was a coincidence. Certainly not! I believe that the Lord chose this spot to reveal the mystery of godly responsibility, the Shechem experience, to us. He wanted to show us that the fastest way into a triumphant destiny is by enduring inconvenience for the sake of His kingdom. Remember it was whilst resting at this spot that He encountered the Samaritan woman who was troubled. Jesus asked for a drink from the unclean.

Here are some principles to keep in mind when thinking about the Shechem experience. When God promised

Abraham and his descendants a land that flows with milk and honey, He was demonstrating that there are two sides to this promise. Honey and milk are the benefits. To have access to these benefits, we need to welcome godly responsibility. Troubles and difficulties are the tools that prepare us to become responsible. Unfortunately, many people welcome the benefits but reject the responsibilities. The elements *'milk'* and *'honey'* are both harvested from animals. As humans, we contribute very little to the production of both milk and honey. I believe these words were carefully chosen by God to teach us the principle that when we learn to depend on Him fully, He in turn releases all the good things we need without the struggle.

The inconveniences we endure in Shechem are nothing compared to the *milk* and *honey* that flow from this wonderful place. Shechem experiences position us to better rely on the supply system of God. Shechem is a place where we can experience God's rest and peace.

THE MEDIUM OF EXCELLENCE: OUR DIVINE DESTINY

It is important for us to understand that the spirit of excellence does not operate in a vacuum. The Apostle Peter says in 1 Peter 2: 9, that as believers, we are a chosen generation called to display Christ's glory and His excellence. The vehicle for exhibiting His excellence is found in the plans He ordained us to fulfill. Embedded in every one of these plans is the spiritual DNA for excellence. We were given access to this genetic code when we accepted Him as our personal Saviour and Lord.

It is important that we acquire a sound biblical understanding of God's plan for ourselves. Destiny equips us with the tools with which we can execute the plan He called us to fulfill. One commonality among the various biblical characters is that God operated in their lives through the different plans He commissioned each one of them to fulfill. However, the extent to which the spirit of excellence was allowed to flourish was dependent on the zeal they had for things of God. God says in the book of Jeremiah,

> *For I know the plans I have for you," declares the LORD, "plans to prosper you and not to harm you, plans to give you hope and a future".*
>
> JEREMIAH 29:11 (NIV)

It is obvious here that in God's mind every human being He creates is commissioned with a destiny. The good news is that every single one of these plans is awesome. Every plan comes with a time frame, a geographic location, and unique gifts for maximum impact. It is vital for us to understand that in God's mind these plans are important. The reason for this is that He designed His plans to operate in a network fashion for the common aim of advancing His Kingdom and His people. Whilst our human instinct at times causes us to concentrate on impact levels, God is always focused on the bigger picture by posing the question of *'the extent His plans for His children are contributing to His Divine Agenda?'*

Therefore, a fulfilled destiny in the mind of God, who created and called us, is a life that is centered on fulfilling an aspect of His bigger agenda. This is embodied in what Jesus Christ referred to as 'the great commission' in Matthew 28:16–20. In other words, the totality of the 'individual' call or purpose is in Christ's instruction to His Apostles and disciples to pursue, before ascending to heaven. This bigger divine agenda is what the Apostle Paul is referring to in 1 Corinthians 3:9 when he refers to *'us (as) being labourers together with God in His vineyard*. Knowing and operating within the specific mandate in accordance to the measure of grace assigned by His purpose for us is what guarantees the excellence of a destiny.

We need to tread the path of destiny in accordance to His purpose in order to access the full measure of His Grace.

Every destiny ordained by God is always expected to advance God's agenda here on earth. The reason for this is because God is a spirit and He created man with a physical body to take charge of His footstool, that is, earth. He willed the earth to us for this simple reason,

> *Then God said, "Let Us make man in Our image, according to Our likeness; let them have dominion over the fish of the sea, over the birds of the air, and over the cattle, over all the earth and over every creeping thing that creeps on the earth."*
>
> GENESIS 1:26 (NKJV)

For God to execute any agenda here on earth—His footstool, He uses a man, a human. This is why every destiny is supposed to be advancing His rulership here on earth and reaching out to His people. Showing love to God's people is fundamentally dear to Him regardless of whether they have a good relationship with Him. The reason that makes every man eligible for the love of God is that we all have the identity of God in us because we are made in His image.

We must come to the place where we understand that we can only achieve destiny and purpose in excellence when we learn to put God's agenda over and above our selfish desires. Each time we understand the place of the bigger picture of God's divine agenda, we position ourselves to be used by God. Shechem situations prepare and keep us in remembrance of His agenda by causing us to maintain focus on Him, His kingdom, and His people, by focusing less on ourselves. This is the understanding that distinguished men like Joseph and Daniel from their contemporaries.

2

EXCELLENCE IN THE MAKING: JOSEPH'S STORY

Armed with the understanding of *Shechem* as the spiritual experience and/or location where the optimum environment for the birthing of the spirit of excellence is created, we will proceed with looking closely at the formative years of the life of Joseph with the aim of understanding some deeper truths about attracting the spirit of excellence. The spirit of excellence, once acquired and cultivated, exponentially accelerates the journey to our God-given destiny.

WELCOME YOUR TEST OF RESPONSIBILITY

The Book of Jeremiah tells us that God's plans for us are good, and are to bring us to an expected end (Jeremiah 29:11). However, there is always a price to pay for this greatness.

This price is godly responsibility. In 2 Timothy 2:20–21, the Apostle Paul puts it this way,

> *But in a great house there are not only vessels of gold and silver, but also of wood and clay, some for honor and some for dishonor. Therefore if anyone cleanses himself from the latter, he will be a vessel for honor, sanctified and useful for the Master, prepared for every good work.*
>
> (NKJV)

In other words, the level at which we are prepared to accept godly responsibility determines whether we become highflyers, or failures in life. The cleansing agent discussed in this scripture is what I refer to as trials and difficulties. God will only allow trials to come our way because He knows they may cause discomfort but they can't hurt us. As believers, we will always need divine cleansing and purification. Joseph demonstrated traits of godly responsibility in his formative years in a manner that was unrivalled by both his fathers and siblings. There are some important lessons to learn from the footprints left by this great man of God. Genesis 37:2 states that,

> *… Joseph, being seventeen years old, was feeding the flock with his brothers. And the lad was with the sons of Bilhah and the sons of Zilpah, his father's wives; and Joseph brought a bad report of them to his father …*
>
> (NKJV)

In the Hebrew custom, boys attain maturity at the age of seventeen. Hebrew young men start exhibiting the art of responsibility through tasks assigned by parents. The Bible clearly states that Joseph brought a bad report about his brothers to his father Jacob. This bad report did not come as a surprise at all, given that it concerned the sons Jacob had with his slave wives, Dan, Naphtali, Gad, and Asher. These sons did not seek to protect their father's interests because they probably knew they were not heirs to Jacob's inheritance.

The surprising part, however, is the fact that it was Joseph, even though he was younger in age (Genesis 30:2–13), who brought his brothers' irresponsible behaviour to the attention of their father Jacob. Here, Joseph embodied the role and assumed the responsibility of an older son, an heir to the inheritance. He saw an opportunity to show responsibility, and he took advantage of it. Joseph's action demonstrated to his father that his shoulders were being developed to handle the burdens of others.

Wrapped within every test of responsibility is an opportunity for a glorious life.

Many folk within the body of Christ today believe that God's favour on their lives is what attracts the spirit of excellence, causing it to function by bringing them to heights they aspire without any personal input. Whilst there is partial truth to this assertion, the complete truth is that there is a dimension to the spirit of excellence that is activated when self-interests give way to God's will. That is, people who welcome godly responsibility are the vessels that God fills with the Spirit of Excellence for the sole purpose of executing His agenda, and not their personal interests.

David is one such character in the Bible who mastered the art of accepting godly responsibility even from a very young age. We know that perhaps the circumstances of rejection surrounding David's birth, through to his formative years, would have left him feeling overlooked, especially given that his parents saw him as a reproach. No wonder he was confined to the back side of the desert.

The negative circumstances surrounding David's birth and his formative life was his *Shechem experience*. It was his test of responsibility before his parents. On the one hand, young David identified these unfortunate events as the necessary wilderness environment. He allowed these circumstances to build godly character traits. His shoulders were developed with the capacity to carry the future burdens of God's people via Kingship. He gladly welcomed these burdens without any thought of vendetta toward his parents and siblings. His parents, on the other hand, did not welcome this responsibility. Rather, they despised and frowned at him, failing in this way the test of responsibility. These circumstances restricted David to the backside of the desert, where he was located and from whence he was called by God into his destiny through the Prophet Samuel.

It does not surprise me at all that David would later confront the Philistine giant Goliath who defied the armies of the children of Israel, and welcome in this way a bigger burden. Remember this was the burden his older brothers and compatriots were afraid to confront. Like Joseph, David encountered the wilderness at a young age and gladly welcomed it.

BE A RELIABLE CHILD

Having demonstrated responsibility at a young age, Joseph had proven beyond reasonable doubt that he could handle heavier burdens. It was therefore not surprising that Israel

(Jacob) loved Joseph more than all his sons. The Bible gives the reason for this exceptional love for Joseph as being,

> '... the son of his old age. Also he made him a tunic of many colors'
>
> GENESIS 37:3 (NKJV)

There are two clues that lead us to the revelation hidden in this scripture. It is very unlikely that Israel was talking about loving Joseph purely because he was born to him in his old age. This is because Benjamin was the youngest son. If young age was the reason for expressing this love, Benjamin should have been a better candidate. The age difference between all Israel's sons was within seven years, and so effectively all his sons were born after the age of seventy-seven according to Hebrew historical accounts. The issue of his old age was therefore beside the point. I believe the truth behind Israel's special love for Joseph stemmed from the young man's responsible attitude toward his father. An attitude that was fulfilling the need created by disability due to Israel's advancing age.

In the Hebrew language, the word *son* also means *builder* or one who builds. So Israel's statement in this scripture can also be put this way: *'I love Joseph more than all my other sons because he has proven beyond doubt to be the shoulder I can hold onto at this stage of my old age when I am no longer strong enough to do things for myself'*.

Actions motivated by a good heart attracts the trust of a true father.

Joseph's brothers' attitude toward his dream proved their inability to shoulder responsibility. The Bible says that they became jealous,

> When he told his father as well as his brothers, his father rebuked him and said, "What is this dream you had? Will your mother and I and your brothers actually come and bow down to the ground before you?" **His brothers were jealous of him**, but his father kept the matter in mind.
>
> GENESIS 37:10–11 (NIV)

Jealousy is a symptom of putting self-interest above all. By behaving thus, Joseph's brothers demonstrated to their father Israel that their hearts were full of hate. They were communicating to their father Jacob that they could not be the shoulder he could rely on in his old age.

We can see from scripture that while Jacob's response suggests he didn't fully understand the spiritual intricacies of his son's dream, he kept it in mind. He kept meditating on it so that he could obtain a clearer understanding.

ENCOUNTER THE CERTAIN MAN

Hatred for a vessel God intends to use will always insulate a potential victim, protecting him from harm. As a matter of fact, the more a person is maligned, the more they are elevated.

What was Joseph's crime in this matter? What exactly warranted such hatred? It was the coat of many colours given to him by his father. This gift made Joseph's brothers outrageously jealous of him. In the midst of all this, Joseph was tasked with checking on the welfare of these jealous brothers and even then he didn't refuse,

> *Now his brothers had gone to graze their father's flocks near Shechem, and Israel said to Joseph, "As you know, your brothers are grazing the flocks near Shechem. Come, I am going to send you to them. "Very well," he replied. So he said to him, "Go and see if all is well with your brothers and with the flocks, and bring word back to me." Then he sent him off from the Valley of Hebron ...*
>
> GENESIS 37:12-14 (NIV)

This task was more challenging than the previous one in many regards. Here, he didn't offer to go on his own volition. He was sent by his father. His brothers' hatred toward him was obvious at this stage, and yet he went.

Consider a number of intriguing questions pertaining to the principles of excellence.

Why would Israel send a son he loved into such a volatile situation? Especially given his awareness of the hatred his older sons had for his beloved. Could he not have sent any one of his servants on this mission to protect his son Joseph from potential danger? Especially since we are told he was not without the necessary resources as he possessed wealth both materially and by way of servants.

The one thing we need to understand is that at this stage of Israel's life, well after his encounter with the angel, he had become more spiritual in his actions, and could sense through revelation that the responsibility he was assigning Joseph was the launching pad to fulfilling his divine destiny. This was not solely for Joseph's personal benefit, but for the benefit of the rest of his family.

The second task assigned to Joseph was also an attestation by Israel that he had lost confidence in his older sons Reuben, Simeon, Levi, and Judah. They did not prove themselves worthy of enduring the wilderness of Shechem. Israel had to send Joseph, the son who understood responsibility, to ensure the welfare of his brothers. Amazingly, the result of this well intended effort, despite unleashing the hatred of his brothers, turned out to be a blessing in disguise for Joseph.

Why would Joseph agree to go and seek the welfare of the brothers he knew hated him? And to make matters worse, why was he sent from the valley of Hebron, the place of particularly difficult challenges, to the location of his assignment which was Shechem? I believe Joseph must have been inspired by his son's selfless desire to ensure the welfare of others, regardless of how he was treated. This is the mark of a true champion.

It is unclear at this stage whether Joseph had a revelation about the link this task had with his destiny. The one thing that is certain from Joseph's posture was the unflinching faith he had in his God. This was the faith that guided his walk with God through the *valley of Hebron* to Shechem until he encountered the 'Certain Man',

> *Now a **certain man** found him, and there he was, wandering in the field. And the man asked him, saying, "What are you seeking?" So he said, "I am seeking my brothers. Please tell me where they are feeding their flocks." And the man said, "They have departed from here, for I heard them say, 'Let us go to Dothan.' " So Joseph went after his brothers and found them in Dothan.*
>
> GENESIS 37:15–17 (NKJV)

There are several mysteries concealed in this scripture. First, Joseph's encounter with the entity described in this text as a 'Certain Man' was not a random person, but our Lord Jesus Christ. We know that Joseph's brothers were in Shechem long before he was sent there to look for them. The question that arises here is, why did Joseph's brothers not have an encounter with the same man? Especially given that the scripture tells us that 'The Man' told Joseph that his brothers had departed Shechem and had proceeded to Dothan.

Jesus is more present during our trials and battles, but our hurts often make Him invisible.

Isn't it amazing that in our walk with God as believers we can sometimes get distracted by menial activities that end up denying us the divine encounters that have been orchestrated to point us toward the path of our destinies? I am sure that when Joseph's brothers met 'This Man', they did not notice Him, let alone have an encounter with Him. I imagine they would have been too busy with issues pertaining to their self-interest, making it impossible to tap into the supernatural. They did not understand the seasons and promptings of divinity, thereby missing a precious opportunity.

When we take a second look at Joseph's encounter with the entity described in this text as *'Certain Man'*, two strange exchanges become evident. I describe these exchanges as strange for the following reasons:

The text informs us that *The Man* found Joseph wandering in the field. This presupposes that it was not Joseph's physical effort that attracted *The Man*, but rather, I believe, that it was the pure state of Joseph's heart and the love with which he was wandering in the field seeking the welfare of others, that attracted *The Man* towards him.

When *The Man* got closer to Joseph, it was *He* who asked Joseph what his problem was, and not the other way round.

Whenever our actions are motivated by a genuine heart and a love for our God and other people, we set ourselves up to receive from His throne room of Grace. When Joseph finally made his demands known to The Man and trusted His ability to solve his problem, The Man provided exactly what Joseph needed by way of direction.

Here, *The Man* saw Joseph's faith in Him and responded with a solution. This is the same for us as believers in Christ today. In our times of trouble, if we only humble ourselves and call on His name, He will hear us and meet us at our point of need. It therefore surprises me to see believers run away from His presence during challenging times. Our moments of trial are opportunities to run into His presence. His name is the strong tower that fills us.

The second mystery in the text has to do with the frustrating circumstances under which Joseph was wandering in the field of Shechem in search of his brothers. Why did Joseph not return home after his rescue effort became complicated? Joseph had a good reason, but he decided to stay in the wilderness, pressing hard for the welfare of his haters. This is the mark of godly responsibility.

Joseph had two fundamental pathways to choose from. One was that of exercising godly responsibility and the other, taking the path of least resistance, that of convenience, pleasing the self. We know from scripture that he chose that of godly responsibility. It was with the selfless heart of seeking the interests of others that Joseph encountered *The Man* I believe was Jesus Christ our Lord, who led him towards Egypt and his destiny.

Here are some principles hidden in this mystery.

- It is in the process of wandering around the wilderness of Shechem, of responsibility, that we experience our divine encounters. There is always a price to pay for those encounters. In any wilderness situation we face, we must pay the price with trials and battles in order to exchange our troubles with His divine revelations. This was what Joseph's brothers missed in Shechem.

- As Christians, whenever we embark on a project or a journey in life, we must always ask ourselves what the true motivation is behind what we do. That is, if the motivation for doing what we do is to embellish our self-interest, then we are without doubt on the path of failure, in much the same way Joseph's brothers were.

FAVOUR ATTRACTS YOUR DESTINY HELPERS

The Bible's narrative of the slave boy Joseph in the house of Potiphar is nothing short of the manifestation of God's favour. Genesis 39:3 says that the favour around Joseph was so conspicuous that even his pagan master Potiphar noticed that, *"the Lord was with him and that the Lord gave him success in everything he did"* as a result, *"Joseph found favour in his eyes and became his attendant"* (Genesis 39:3-4). This favour did two things for Joseph, it attracted the attention of his master Potiphar and it made Potiphar draw Joseph closer to himself through the medium of service.

Whilst the word *favour* is being used here to characterise the life of Joseph for the first time in the Bible, I want to submit that the favour on Joseph's life did not begin in Potiphar's house. It actually started in Dothan when he was thrown into the pit, before he was sold to the Ishmaelites and Midianites. The word Dothan in the Hebrew language means two wells. Surprisingly, Joseph's brothers did not realise that there were two wells in Dothan. They were only familiar with the dry well (the pit Joseph was thrown into) but had no idea about the other well, which I believe, had water in it. The lesson here is that anytime we walk the walk of godly responsibility, our enemies might think they can overpower us because we may look vulnerable. What they don't know is that there is always a second well we have access to which is not as dry as the first. This well is what I want to refer to as the *reservoir of destiny helpers that* you need in your life. In Joseph's case, he needed the Ishmaelites to take him to Egypt.

The place called Dothan also had something to do with seeing, having divine visions. We remember that this was the place where Joseph's brothers rested and it was while they were breaking bread that they saw the Ishmaelites coming from Gilead on their way to Egypt (Genesis 37:25). Dothan was also the place where the Prophet Elisha calmed his servant who was frightened by the might of the Aramean army, by revealing the vision to him in 2 Kings 6:17. Here it is vital to understand the background to Joseph's favour that so characterised his destiny. We are informed by the scriptures that as soon as Joseph discovered his brothers' location in Dothan and met them, they stripped him of his coat of many colours and put him in a pit (Genesis 37:23). Here is where the divine exchange occurred:

- The coat of many colours was swapped for a coat of favour.
- The empty and dry well was the magnetic force that enabled him to perpetually attract destiny helpers.

The interesting bargaining chip for this divine exchange was the love and good tidings that Joseph brought with him to his brothers. The curses that plagued the lives of Joseph's brothers later were due to the hatred that they'd directed at Joseph in Dothan.

The surprising aspect of this exchange has to do with what happened in the immediate aftermath of this incident.

The scripture says that while Joseph was in the well and the brothers sat down to eat that they looked up and saw the Ishmaelites and Midianites coming from Gilead. This was when the decision to sell Joseph came up.

Although not specifically mentioned in scriptures, I believe that Joseph's act of generosity by way of bringing his brothers food supplies, was the very thing that inspired Judah to come up with the idea of selling Joseph to the merchants. Judah himself may not have had any idea of the calibre of people these merchants were, but I believe God knew that even though Joseph would have felt troubled at that time, he needed to be in the company of people who understood what it meant to be mistreated or betrayed. I believe Joseph needed people who would heal him from the afflictions he suffered whilst in the pit, and these merchants would have given Joseph emotional support.

We know from biblical accounts that the Ishmaelites and Midianites are descendants of Abraham's marital relationships with Hagar and Keturah (Genesis 16:4, and 25:2). This group of people understood rejection. It is no wonder then, that when Moses was fleeing the wrath of Pharaoh after murdering the Egyptian, he fled to the house of Jethro the priest where he sought refuge (Exodus 2:15–16). Therefore, we can conclude that it was Joseph's association with these people that was the first show of God's favour in his life. Favour was activated because the Ishmaelites were returning from Gilead, which was a place consecrated to the things of God. The scripture says that their camels were carrying spices, balm, and myrrh which represent healing and comfort for the hurt and distressed (Jeremiah 8:22).

It is believed that Gilead was one of the cities considered a safe haven for troubled people (Joshua 20:7–8). Among the many other reasons these merchants would have gone to Gilead would have been to deal with their troubles. I can imagine that being in the company of these merchants, Joseph would have been encouraged by their positive words. Choosing to focus on the positive side of life rather than the negative. Encouraging words help heal emotional wounds inflicted on us and lighten the burden of our afflictions. Encouraging words talk us into our destiny rather than talk us out of our destiny. People who offer such words of encouragement are destiny helpers. These are the kinds of people we need to have around us whenever we feel let down by others. These were the destiny helpers around Joseph on his way to Egypt.

UPGRADE YOUR FAVOUR

Joseph encountered a *Certain Man*, Jesus Christ, in Shechem and the direction of his destiny was changed for the better, albeit, wrapped in a package of myriad challenges. Although at this stage his coat of many colours had been stripped off of him by his brothers out of envy and bitterness, Joseph received a superior coat as a result of his encounter with the Lord.

Amazingly, his brothers were too carnal to understand that merely stripping him of that coat could not prevent his dreams from coming to fruition. Furthermore, Joseph's '*coat of many colours*' had metamorphosed into what I term as the '*coat of favour*'. The coat of favour attracted his master Potiphar's attention. Potiphar's household became infected with the power of this coat. Potiphar's wife was seriously infected by it, to the extent that she wanted to connect to this favour, but unfortunately, in a carnal way, because she was Egyptian and did not have a covenant with Jehovah God.

Notice what she said when she realised that her attempts at connecting to Joseph's coat of favour proved futile,

> *And so it was, when she saw that **he had left his garment in her hand and fled outside**, that she called to the men of her house and spoke to them, saying, "See, he has **brought in to us a Hebrew to mock us**. He came into me to lie with me, and I cried out with a loud voice.*
> GENESIS 39:13-14 (NKJV)

Joseph was making the statement that, *'You cannot connect to a blessing that is reserved for Hebrews as long as you want to remain Egyptian'*. Potiphar's wife attempted negotiating for favour from the God of the Hebrews but wanted to remain Egyptian and pagan. Joseph was familiar with these kinds of tricks. I can imagine Joseph saying to himself, *'I know your kind'*. Joseph was well informed of similar incidents that had occurred in the history of his family. He knew that Mrs. Potiphar's kindness concealed cunning, the sole purpose of which is always to blind the children of God in order to manipulate and derail them from the path of their destiny.

Favour can take you where intellect, strength, or skill may not.

Surely, Joseph must have been acting on godly faith at this point. We see this when he backed himself when faced with the temptation of Potiphar's wife. He could've succumbed given that hewas lonely, a slave boy in a foreign land, and had been rejected by his brothers, but he didn't. Joseph understood one thing well, that his boss Potiphar had put

Joseph in charge of everyone in the house except Potiphar's wife, and such as the hierarchy was, she was not Joseph's responsibility nor was she under Joseph's covering.

This faith motivated action, landed Joseph in an Egyptian jail, which became Joseph's own wilderness experience. Here, he would meet a congregation of people who desperately needed his God-given strengths. A crucial lesson that believers in Christ can learn from this episode in Joseph's life is that matters that do not pertain to our calling are not our responsibility. This is purely because when indulged they tend to be the very things that are most likely to keep us away from our divine destiny or even destroy us. Joseph knew this secret, as was recorded in his response to his master's wife in Genesis 39:9. We have to identify our boundaries and stay within them.

Whatever position of responsibility we find ourselves in, we must always keep in mind that we are not there to serve our own purpose, but rather to make ourselves available to be used in executing God's agenda. Joseph mastered this secret to the extent that even though his resolve landed him in jail, he was not bitter nor did he harbour anger toward those who falsely accused him. The spirit of peace that was working in his life in those circumstances eventually compelled him to become an instrument of comfort to his fellow prisoners who were troubled, and who in turn ended up becoming instrumental to his emancipation and elevation.

CARE FOR THE DISTRESSED

The writer of Genesis says that,

> '... the captain of the [prison] charged Joseph with [some of the prisoners], and he served them ...'
>
> GENESIS 40:4 (NKJV)

There is no doubt that Joseph's time in prison was probably the darkest period in his life, made worse by the fact that he was accused of a crime he had not committed and that as a slave boy in a foreign land he had no support system. Furthermore, due to his status, he was denied defense and was subsequently denied a fair trial before he was thrown into jail indefinitely. In such challenging and trying circumstances, only the fact that he was a person with the godly kind of faith and in full possession of the spirit of endurance, was he enabled to be an agent of encouragement who embodied a positive demeanour whilst in prison. The Bible according to Genesis 40:6–7 says,

> And Joseph came in to them in the morning and looked at them, and saw that they were sad. So he asked Pharaoh's officers who were with him in the custody of his lord's house saying, "Why do you look so sad today?"
>
> (NKJV)

Notice here that it was Joseph who took the initiative to approach his depressed colleagues and inquire of their troubles. Also notice Joseph's response to them when they shared their problem. He identified and declared to them the source of his divine ability to overcome, even before making demands on this ability. The writer of Genesis does not reveal the specific offence these prisoners committed beyond the fact that they offended Pharaoh (Genesis 40:1–3).

> **Seasons that render us vulnerable are the actual building blocks of a dynamic destiny. Don't shun them, but rather embrace them.**

However unfair their offence may have been, it is clear that Joseph's punishment for his alleged offence was more unjust than theirs. Yet, they all ended up in prison anyway, and guess who was troubled? Joseph was undoubtedly in a position to be more troubled, given the nature of his indictment and the fact that he'd been imprisoned for a longer period of time. Yet he was the one comforting them. What a heart of endurance Joseph displayed!

As believers in Christ Jesus, this is the heart we need to possess to attract the spirit of excellence. It is surprising to see that some believers in the faith today fail this test of endurance in the face of tribulations that the Apostle Paul talked about in Romans 5:3–4. We need to overcome the hurt to self to be able to handle the burdens of others. This is a vital cost, and we must pay it in full if we are to experience a speedy ascent into the great destiny God has planned for us.

> **In the race to our destinies, let us eschew bitterness, anger, pride, jealousy, lies, etc.**

GALLOP INTO YOUR DESTINY

No matter the kind of tribulation you encounter on your way, in your walk with God, as long as you keep the faith you stay focused on doing His will., He will thenconnect you to a Pharaoh in your life who will embellish your coat of favour by elevating you from a place of obscurity to prominence (Genesis 41:42). As Jesus stated in Matthew 5:16, you will be enabled to, *'Let your light so shine before men, that they may see your good works and glorify your Father in heaven.'* (NKJV). This was the light that was radiating from the life of Joseph in the land of Egypt. Joseph's light was so bright that the darkness around Pharaoh, his wise men, and all the people of Egypt could not comprehend it. This was the light that shone the light of hope in the darkness that surrounded Pharaoh and his perplexing dream.

Joseph was the only one in his family to have accomplished this journey to destiny in the shortest possible time frame. It was within thirteen years as we will see in the subsequent chapters of this book. Joseph's quick ascent to prominence and destiny was not by chance but by intentionally overcoming challenging situations in the wilderness called Shechem. A wilderness where he confronted difficulties in his life either by choice or divine providence and where he underwent preparation for higher godly responsibilities. Joseph always welcomed these challenges and did not shun them. He stayed pure throughout, maintaining a loving heart and cultivating an enduring spirit. This was where his father and siblings fell short.

I am not for the idea of orchestrating drama and self-inflicting trouble and/or tribulations in an attempt to reach destiny quickly. What I want us to understand here is that sometimes it is the will of God for us to go through trials and tribulations for the sole purpose of purging us of what the Apostle Paul described as our 'excess weights' when he said,

> 'Therefore, since we are surrounded by such a great cloud of witnesses, let us throw off everything that hinders and the sin that so easily entangles. And let us run with perseverance the race marked out for us'
> HEBREWS 12:1 (NKJV)

The wilderness is the place where we can focus solely on God with the solitary purpose of getting to know Him personally rather than learning about Him through other people, as Paul inferred when talking about 'going to Arabia after his encounter on the road to Damascus, instead of going to Jerusalem' in Galatians 1:17. The wilderness is a place where you can build godly character, endurance, and a heart with the capacity for responsibility. It is a place where one can ask 'why' but not a place to complain. Passing this test requires reliance on God's time-table for endurance till exit, and not on our own time-table.

We must always understand that God allows us to go through wilderness situations, our personal Shechem, so that our thought patterns, speech, and actions will be seasoned with His flavour. As such, we can consequently be trusted by heaven with bigger responsibilities within God's divine agenda. The wilderness is a place where the desires of the flesh are purged to make way for a selfless heart.

We know that God is 'all knowing' and has 'ultimate wisdom' (1 Corinthians 2:7), He knows that whenever an opportunity is upon us, it is too late to begin preparing for it, so in His ultimate wisdom God chooses to prepare us in advance, in the place we call the wilderness, Shechem. In the wild we are cut off from every ungodly distraction, allowing us the time and space to become well prepared for performing wonders in the destiny plans He ordained for us. The earlier we understand this, the earlier we can arrive at our destiny.

3

SHORTEN YOUR WALK TO DESTINY: LESSONS FROM ABRAHAM

In the previous chapter, we saw how the spirit of excellence was ignited and then planted in the fertile ground of Joseph's life in order to flourish. We saw how this great man of God was confronted in varying degrees with complex circumstances, and in some instances, temptations warranting a difficult choice. Despite the challenge, he made the best of every situation. We saw how he allowed the love and faith in his God to eventually guide him into the fullness of his destiny in the span of just thirteen years.

Yet, Abraham, who is considered one of the most important icons of our faith, according to Hebrews 11:11-12, and is very often accredited the title "father of faith" due to the closeness of his relationship with God, did not respond promptly to God's call to relocate. Further on in this chapter we will see how Abraham's initial hesitation—with regard to exercising the power of headship of his household in allowing Sarai his wife and Lot his nephew to slow his walk with God—impacted God's overall plan for his life. Whilst these actions or inactions on the part of Abraham did not in any way terminate the plan God destined for him, they contributed in one way or another to unnecessary delays in reaching his destiny.

Our aim in this chapter is to learn certain truths about specific lines we are to draw in the sand of our Christian lives if we truly want to nurture the spirit of excellence to fast track arrival at our destiny.

DON'T STRAY FROM YOUR BETHEL

We have seen how God encouraged Abraham upon his arrival in Shechem with the generous promise made to him and his descendants according to Genesis 12:6-7. The question we need to ask ourselves here, is why God decided to appear to Abraham only after he arrived in Shechem. Was this incident a mere coincidence or was God making a point? I believe that God was prompting Abraham to dwell in Shechem rather than to just sojourn there. Notice the promise of God in Genesis 12:7,

> 'Then the Lord appeared to Abram and said, "To your descendants I will give this land." And there he built an altar to the Lord, who had appeared to him'.
>
> GENESIS 12:7 (NKJV)

In this place, God promised to give Abraham's descendants the lands around Shechem. God's focus on Abraham's descendants suggests that He was thinking long-term. Abraham appears to have understood God's long-term mindset demonstrated by his building of an altar, before moving further east to put up his tent near Bethel (Genesis

12:8). And yet, we learn in the subsequent verse, Abraham and his household actually relocated to Egypt after that because of a famine. I wonder whether he consulted God regarding the troubles caused by this famine before embarking on a journey to Egypt. Even if we assume that he did, the question is, was he patient enough to wait for an answer from God?

As believers in Christ, we often find ourselves in similar challenging situations where we also fail to seek the counsel of God before taking action. It may have been that the famine was to be the wilderness situation God wanted to purposefully lead Abraham into to prepare him for a shorter route to the fulfillment of his destiny.

We are familiar with the consequence of Abraham's misguided action when he was in the land of Egypt; God had to rescue him from the hand of Pharaoh. The point I want to make here is that Abraham had no business going to Egypt in the first place. It seems that the entire period he spent in Egypt was wasted time. He possessed comprehensive knowledge of the destiny God had planned for him, especially that he was the seed bearer of God's blessing (Genesis 22:18, Galatians 3:8) so he could have effortlessly shortened his arrival at this great destiny. Furthermore, when we look at the circumstances that led to Abraham's return to Canaan, we see the hand of God in the rerouting:

> But **the Lord plagued Pharaoh and his house** with great plagues because of Sarai, Abram's wife. And Pharaoh called Abram and said, "What is this you have done to me? Why did you not tell me that she was your wife? Why did you say, 'She is my sister'? I might have taken her as my wife. Now therefore, here is your wife; take her and go your way." So Pharaoh commanded his

men concerning him; and **they sent him away**, *with his wife and all that he had.*

GENESIS 12:17–20 (NKJV)

We see the household of Pharaoh being inflicted with plagues by God Himself, for no other reason but to cause Pharaoh to deport Abraham. Pharaoh was simply working into God's script. Sometimes we need the likes of Pharaoh to redirect us onto the path of destiny.

WATCH OUT FOR YOUR DESTINY HIJACKERS

The fact that God's plans for every one of us are great, does not insulate us from the responsibility of guarding our destiny with diligence. We cannot afford to take our destiny for granted. The stakes are too high! We need to always be on guard. As the Apostle Paul puts it, *'our warfare is not against flesh and blood but against principalities and powers'* (Ephesians 6:12a) operating through people.

> You may succeed in stealing someone's destiny, but don't forget you may lack the grace to accomplish it.

Destiny hijackers come in different shapes and sizes, colours and creeds. Some cause people who are genuinely walking towards their destiny to stumble.

Another kind uses various manipulative strategies to steal the vision of people. They are the masked men of Satan whose main motivation is evil. Whilst some destiny hijackers may not know they are being used as masked men in fighting a proxy war for the devil by propagating his evil agenda against God, others are well aware of what they are doing and are also well aware of the consequences of their wicked agendas. As believers, we need to be cautious of these kinds of characters if we want to see the great destiny God has ordained for us fulfilled in the shortest possible time.

The narrative in Genesis 11:31 gives an account of the relocation of Terah's family from Ur of the Chaldeans to Haran, after the death of his eldest son Haran. The scripture infers that Terah's original intention was to go to Canaan. However, after arriving in Haran, the scripture says that Terah decided to settle there with his family.

There are two important points that Moses, the writer of the book of Genesis leaves unclarified in this narrative:

1. The main reason Terah decided to relocate his family. There must have been a trigger resulting in the making of this critical decision.
2. The reason he decided to settle in the city of Haran rather than adhering to his originally intended destination.

In order to understand what is going on here, we must dive deeply into other scriptures. In the book of Genesis we read that,

> Now the Lord had said to Abram: Get out of your country, From your family And from your father's house To a land that I will show you.
>
> GENESIS 12:1 (NKJV)

It is obvious from the rendering of this scripture that the Lord had already spoken to Abram (Abraham) prior to Terah's decision to move his family from Ur, or at least before the family settled in Haran. When we look at the revelation given by Stephen the Elder, we get a clearer picture of the narrative Moses was presenting. In Acts 7:1–4, Stephen points out that,

> '... The God of glory appeared to our father Abraham when he was in Mesopotamia, before he dwelt in Haran, and said unto him, "Get out of your country and from your relatives and come to a land that I will show you." Then he came out of the land of the Chaldeans and dwelt in Haran. And from there, when his father was dead, he moved him to this land which you now dwell.
>
> ACTS 7:2–4 (NKJV)

Here we see how God revealed to Abraham the plan He had, but for some reason this plan ended up being executed by his father Terah. I wonder how Terah came to know of this plan? Who could have told him, and why didn't Abraham act on the instruction promptly?

This is the predicament many believers find themselves in today. We receive wonderful revelations and/or prophecies about our destinies, and instead of immediately acting on the instructions that accompany these divine visitations, we tell family members and friends who in turn respond with attempts to subvert our plans.

The truth about destiny is that every destiny is unique. Every single one is packaged together with a unique ability and special grace which has been intricately wired into the individual God entrusts with it in its entirety. Many people, and sadly sometimes even believers, try to hijack destinies without possessing the grace, gifts, and evidence in the way of scars. That is, evidence of the fulfillment of the requirements of preparation necessary to bring these plans to fruition according to the perfect will of our Lord as He has ordained. No wonder Terah ended up abandoning his original plan upon arriving in the city of Haran. Abraham's initial hesitation to act on God's voice prolonged his destiny for the entire period he dwelt in Haran, that is until God spoke to him the second time.

The principles we learn from this narrative are that whenever we give destiny hijackers room in our lives, we automatically default to the requirement to sit the exam again. Even though we should have already qualified to fulfill impactful destinies the first time. We also delay destinies that are connected to ours when we give destiny hijackers opportunity, and we cause discrepancies in the divine agenda which has previously been set in motion by God Himself.

NEGOTIATE YOUR WAY AROUND TRANSIT POSTS

Let's revisit a statement I made in chapter one regarding the destinies God planned for every one of us. God specifically designed these unique destinies to fit into His master plan, His divine agenda, in a network fashion. The interconnectedness and simultaneous working of these destinies is what brings perfection in His divine agenda here. This is why He assigns destiny helpers to every destiny He commissions.

Unfortunately, due to possessing the ability to transform himself into an angel of light (2 Corinthians 11:14), our enemy Satan understands this divine order through which God's master plan operates. This is why he sends people I refer to as destiny wreckers our way. The main agenda of these kinds of people is to disrupt the divine order. They achieve this by diverting us from the path of destiny through diabolical means. They sow seeds of discord.

> **Transit post are designed to provide us direction towards destiny and not to give us a reason to settle.**

The Bible tells us that when Terah left Ur with his family, he arrived at the city of Haran and decided to settle there, instead of continuing to Canaan which was the original destination he had in mind (Genesis 11:31). In Genesis 11:28, we are told that Haran, one of Terah's sons, died whilst the family was still in the city of Ur.

Whilst the Bible doesn't clarify what the circumstances that caused the relocation of Terah and his family from the city of Ur definitively were, biblical scholars indicate that the death of his son Haran played a vital role in his decision to move. For Terah, the name Haran became synonymous with tragedy and pain. It was therefore that very wound which hadn't yet healed prior to him embarking on his journey that grounded him when he arrived at the city of Haran. The lesson here is that we cannot afford to carry our hurts with us on our walk to destiny. Hurt is the excess baggage we must offload in order to hasten our journey to destiny.

No wonder that upon arriving in Haran, he settled there instead of sojourning. He obviously sought solace in the many provisions available in that city. Terah chose the comforts he found in Haran over the destiny he hijacked. This is what happens when we steal other's destinies.

DEALING WITH THE LOT KIND

When God called Abraham (Genesis 12:1), the one thing He made clear was that Abraham was to leave his comfort zone, his country, and his family. It surprises me that Abraham decided to take Lot on this journey. I can understand that since Lot was a young orphan Abraham may have felt obligated as Lot's responsible uncle.

We know that Lot was the biological son of Haran, Abraham's brother. Being the only son of Haran, Lot was a reminder of his late father to the Terah family. However, Haran symbolised the excess baggage in the way of grief and pain that Terah hadn't dealt with before leaving Ur. This unresolved hurt became the cause of Terah's abandonment of the vision of going to Canaan as he opted to settle in the city of Haran. As the son of Haran, Lot became the incarnate excess baggage Abraham should have dealt with before departing the city of Haran. Abraham failed to deal with this baggage, out of ignorance perhaps, and the consequences came to bear heavily.

'The Lot' kind of people are materialistic, and always seeking temporary comforts. They will sacrifice everything for anything that gives them comfort. As believers, we need to be careful of the way we relate to this kind of folk. Notice the strange rivalry that arose between uncle and nephew soon after Abraham and Lot became wealthy in Genesis 13:7-8,

> *And there was strife between the herdsmen of Abram's livestock and the herdsmen of Lot's livestock. The Canaanites and the Perizzites then dwelt in the land. So Abram said to Lot, "Please let there be no strife*

> *between you and me, and between my herdsmen and your herdsmen; for we are brethren.*
> GENESIS 13:7-8 (NKJV)

I believe that Lot's material prosperity was achieved by virtue of associating with Abraham—The Blessed. Yet, Lot ended up fighting the very source of his prosperity.

Destiny ties are deeper than blood ties. In our walk to destiny, the priority should be destiny ties.

I wonder why there was no tension between the two men when they both had fewer material possessions. It is evident from the tone of Abraham's response in Genesis 13:7-8 that Lot's carnal mentality triggered this tension. He was obviously envious of his uncle's wealth and would have poisoned the minds of the herdsmen. We should also note that when Lot was asked to choose between the lands, he chose the valley of Jordan where the pastures were greener and where there was an abundance of water (Genesis 13:9-10). Carnal minded people are always attracted to material things. These kinds of people cannot be destiny helpers, but rather destiny wreckers.

We need to be careful of the kinds of people we keep in our inner circle if we desire a brisk walk into destiny. Family or friendship ties do not necessarily automatically predispose people to connect to our destiny. Consider on the one hand, young David who had no blood tie with Jonathan, yet on the spiritual level Jonathan was David's destiny helper.

In much the same way, John the Baptist was a destiny helper to Jesus Christ, in-spite of their blood tie (Luke 1:35–36).

WAIT FOR YOUR ISAAC

In chapter one we learned how God ordains destiny to us individually, and how these destinies are designed to work in a network manner within His master plan, His kingdom agenda. We are all aware of the great victories God brought to Abraham prior to his encountering Melchizedek the King of Salem, and the subsequent promise God made to Abraham,

> *After these things the word of the Lord came to Abram in a vision, saying, "Do not be afraid, Abram. I am your shield, your exceedingly great reward."*
>
> GENESIS 15:1 (NKJV)

Immediately after this promise, Abraham proceeded with a request to God without consulting his wife Sarai. After having walked with God all this time, Abraham knew that whenever God promises a 'great reward', it's like He opens a blank cheque to whoever He is dialoguing with to name his or her request. Abraham went on to make a request for a son, a desire that was so dear to his heart. Notice how God responded to this request,

> *Then He brought him outside and said, "Look now toward heaven, and count the stars if you are able to number them." And He said to him, "So shall your descendants be."*
>
> GENESIS 15:5 (NKJV)

The point here is that Sarai was not privy to Abraham's dialogue with God. She was not party to the picture God showed Abraham. She was unaware right up until the deal was concluded, according to Genesis 15:6. I believe that God excluded Sarai from this dialogue for very good reasons. It is therefore surprising for Abraham, who was signatory to the deal through his faith which made him right with God according to Genesis 15:6, to be swayed by Sarai's whisperings later,

> *So Sarai said to Abram, "See now, the Lord has restrained me from bearing children. Please, go in to my maid; perhaps I shall obtain children by her." And Abram heeded the voice of Sarai.*
>
> GENESIS 16:2 (NKJV)

I can understand why Sarai whispered an idea that was contrary to the will of God to her husband Abraham. What beats my imagination is why would Abraham entertained this strange voice after having experienced such an awesome visitation by God Himself. Notice that the very words Sarai used, "*The Lord has not allowed me to have children*" aligned with the picture God showed Abraham when he led him outside, "*Your descendants will be too many to count like the stars you see*".

We are all familiar with the costly price Abraham paid as a direct result of acting on this strange voice. Oftentimes we become surrounded by all manner of people whispering many different things to us. Often these whisperings do not line up with the destiny God has planned for us. Surprisingly, it is often the people who are closest to us who tend to cast aspersions on what God has said. We are all aware of the whisperings of Job's wife in his moment of difficulty in Job 2:9–10, which were in direct contrast to the agenda of heaven for Job.

Isn't it surprising that the very Sarai who suggested that Abraham have sexual intercourse with her slave girl Hagar in order to have a child which would continue the Abrahamic bloodline and inheritance (Genesis 16:2); would be the very child Sarai would later refer to as a *'born servant'* who must not inherit? What a contradiction! The Sarai kind of people are usually inconsistent and tend to be motivated by self-interest. They are often doubtful of what God can do (Genesis 18:11–15).

No wonder Sarai, like the rest of Joseph's ancestors, ended up being buried in the tomb at the "Cave of Machpelah" together with Abraham, Isaac, Rebekah, Jacob, and Leah. I refer to these six people as failures in the light of the spirit of excellence. The reason for this is that they all had wonderful opportunities to experience an unhindered walk into their destinies in the excellence God had ordained for them, but they failed.

Faith by itself may unlock the door of God's permissible will, but faith that works through patience unleashes God's perfect will.

It is also important to emphasise that sometimes people allow themselves to be used as a means for transmitting and superimposing strange voices onto God's divine agenda. I have seen powerful men of God allow themselves to be used this way. A notable example is when our Lord Jesus was giving a hint to His disciples about how He was to go about the business of fulfilling his destiny,

> *... Jesus began to show to His disciples that He must go to Jerusalem, and suffer many things from the elders and chief priests and scribes, and be killed, and be raised the third day. Then Peter took Him aside and began to rebuke Him, saying, "Far be it from You, Lord; this shall not happen to You!" But He turned and said to Peter,* **"Get behind Me, Satan! You are an offense to Me, for you are not mindful of the things of God, but the things of men."**
>
> MATHEW 16:21-23 (NKJV)

Isn't it surprising that the Peter who was referred to by Jesus Himself as *'The Rock on which He will build His church'* a few verses back, could be used by the devil to say such a thing? The most shocking aspect of Peter's whisperings is that even though he was given access to divine revelation regarding the true identity of Jesus Christ, *"You are the Christ, son of the living God"* a few moments ago, he was also the vessel the devil used to release venom from the pit of hell.

The paradox is that the rock on which Christ was to build His church against which no gate of hell could prevail, is the same rock the enemy used as a means to transmit lies to Jesus. The lesson to us as the body of Christ is that oftentimes the vessels that God uses to fulfill His agenda can be the vessels the devil pursues to transmit his strange whisperings.

If Peter, of all people, could be used by Satan, then what chance do the rest of us have? We must be very careful to discern every voice of contradiction. Men of God have to be careful not to allow themselves to be used by the enemy to propagate his lies. We need the leading of the Holy Spirit to distinguish between strange whisperings coming from the kingdom of darkness, and direction that comes from hearing the true voice of God. This is why we always need an overflow of the Wonderful Counsellor, the Holy Spirit, to help us flee from the presence of the devil.

4

STAY AWAKE ON YOUR PATH TO DESTINY: ISAAC'S PREDICAMENT

In this chapter, we will look at another aspect of the walk of destiny I call *'spiritual alertness'*. It is only when we examine the reasons God allows trials to intercept us, that understand when we learn the inherent lessons we can then graduate to fulfill the plans God has destined for us.

The journey into destiny is largely spiritual in nature, and can be diametrically opposed to the physical steps we take navigating our everyday life. Here, in exploring the spiritual complexities inherent in our journey into destiny, we will use the legacy of Isaac, which is often described in scripture as *'The Promise'*. We will identify and gain a deeper understanding of the pitfalls we can avoid in order to fulfill our divine purpose in the appointed time frame. Isaac is often credited in scripture as the man who, through faith, acted on the word of God by dwelling and sowing in a land stricken by famine (Genesis 26:2-14).

In this chapter, we will further develop the discussion of the spirit of excellence by focusing specifically on the other side of the life of Isaac. We will take a close look at the costly price Isaac paid for remaining in a spiritual slumber in an environment and in a moment where he was supposed to be spiritually awake and very much in charge in Shechem.

THE PRICE OF CARNALITY

The Bible tells us that Isaac's parents died of old age and in good health. The question that comes to mind here is, what could have been the cause of Isaac's blindness? How could a man described in scripture as so blessed and envied by so many (Genesis 26:14), end up blind to the extent that he was taken advantage of by his wife and younger son?

The prosperity Isaac enjoyed was consistent with the promise God had made to Abraham and his descendants (Genesis 12:6–7). It echoed and resonated in Joseph's life. However, the blindness that befell him in the latter years was inconsistent with the promise by which he was birthed. His blindness must have been caused by something worth exploring here in order to clarify the point. In Genesis 24:67 we learn that,

> *Then Isaac brought her **into his mother Sarah's tent;** and he took Rebekah and she became his wife, and he loved her. **So Isaac was comforted** after his mother's death.*
>
> (NKJV)

Pause here for a moment and reflect on this scripture. Whilst we cannot categorically state with certainty whether he was already rich to the extent we are given to understand in Genesis 26:12–13, one thing that we are sure of is that Isaac was not lacking at the very least in his old age. Isaac's inability to afford to own his own tent, however, remains a mystery to me. Especially given that his father Abraham was rich and could have assisted Isaac with purchasing a tent when he connected him with Rebekah, in much the same way he himself had been provided for as a younger man.

The following question remains, why did Issac have to move into his mother's tent with his bride to feel loved? Here is an example of someone who was unable to demonstrate an ability to deal with the vacuum of isolation. The wilderness is a place of isolation and as such equips us to handle isolation in future circumstances with ease. Compare Isaac's situation here with his grandson Joseph's. Joseph was sold into slavery and was taken to a strange land where he lost hope of ever seeing his family again. To make matters worse, Joseph was unjustly accused and thrown into prison; and yet notwithstanding untenable circumstances he maintained a countenance of joy.

In direct contrast, Isaac was void of joy here. What sort of comfort from his late mother had he become so accustomed to and so dependent on that he could not manage after Sarah died? The void even caused him to defile Sarah's tent in this manner. (Genesis 24:67). Isaac was so devastated and hungry for love that it took the love Rebekah offered him as his wife to calm him. Why could he not fill this vacuum with The Ultimate Love, that of God Himself?

With this foundation, we can say that Isaac's spiritual blindness started at Mount Moriah. In Genesis 22:3, we read that God wanted to test Abraham's faith by instructing him to sacrifice his only son Isaac to Him. Abraham responded by,

> ... *[rising] early in the morning and saddled his donkey, and **took two of his young men with him, and Isaac his***

son; *and he split the wood for the burnt offering, and arose and went to the place of which God had told him.*

GENESIS 22:3 (NKJV)

Initially we see the composition of the team that accompanied Abraham to the mountain of Moriah for the sacrifice. The narrative then concludes with a composition of the team that returned after the burnt offering of the ram was made to God,

*… **Abraham returned to his young men**, and they rose and went together to Beersheba; and Abraham dwelt at Beersheba.*

GENESIS 22:19 (NKJV)

When we have a close look at these two scriptures, we notice that Isaac's name is included in the first trip but is conspicuously missing in the return trip. The question is, where could Isaac have gone and for what reason did he not return with his father Abraham, especially since God had made miraculous provision for the sacrifice by providing the ram? (Genesis 22:12–13).

Spiritual blindness sets in when we don't catch divine revelation.

I believe that Isaac was deeply hurt and would have felt betrayed upon realising his father's intention to sacrifice him. This would have caused him to abscond from Mount Moriah, 'the presence of God', infuriated. To make matters worse, I believe Isaac would have discussed his ordeal with his mother Sarah.

The truth is that Isaac had an extremely rare opportunity to see the manifested presence of God on Mount Moriah, but the seed of hurt that had taken root in him did not allow him to catch this divine revelation. No wonder we don't hear the name Isaac after the Mount Moriah event until he was about to marry Rebekah.

In Genesis 23:1–2, we read that,

*'Sarah lived one hundred and twenty-seven years; these were the years of the life of Sarah. So Sarah died in Kirjath Arba (that is Hebron) in the land of Canaan, and **Abraham came** to mourn for Sarah and to weep for her.'*

(NKJV)

The question of where Sarah was living all this time remains. I would have expected her to continue living with Abraham and Isaac in Beersheba up until the sacrifice at Moriah, just as she did prior to Ishmael and Hagar being thrown out of the house (Genesis 21:1–14), but that was not the case. No wonder Sarah's name was never mentioned again in the Bible up until she died in Hebron, and after Ishmael and Hagar were thrown out (Genesis 23:1–2). The next question therefore is, at what point did she leave Beersheba to go to Hebron? And for what reason? Could there have been a clash of mindsets between her and her husband Abraham? If that is the case, one can conclude that this might have caused the separation between husband and wife.

Amazingly, the mention in Genesis 24:67 of 'Isaac taking Rebekah his wife into his mother Sarah's tent to be comforted after Sarah's death' confirms where Isaac fled to after the event on Mount Moriah. His experience at Moriah pushed him into subscribing to his mother's mindset. No wonder he couldn't handle the vacuum created by his mother's absence.

This kind of mindset makes one a 'mummy's boy' as opposed to a responsible grown man.

Whenever we refuse to learn the lessons of godly responsibility, we surrender our lives to the dictates of others. Who was given the responsibility to go in search of a wife for Isaac? Eliezer of Damascus. Even though he was a servant, he was in charge of Isaac's inheritance (Genesis 24:2), primarily because Isaac had fled from responsibility. Isaac failed to allow the Shechem experience to develop his shoulders. He proved incapable of being in charge of what belonged to him. He took the path of least resistance. He could not endure trials and challenges. Instead of returning home with his father, he fled, and finally settled in southern Canaan (Genesis 24:62).

Many Christians find themselves in a similar predicament today. Instead of seeking continuous spiritual nourishment, we seek temporary, material comfort that provides instant satisfaction by way of fulfilling fleshly desires at the expense of divine revelation, by words of knowledge, and words of wisdom that we need in order to prevail over our enemy Satan.

Isaac's action in Genesis 24:67 brings to mind another show of carnality that made the journey of the children of Israel to the promised land longer than was originally planned by God. The Bible tells us in the book of Exodus that,

> *'Then it came to pass, when Pharaoh had let the people go, that* **God did not lead them by way of the land of the Philistines, although that was near;** *for God said, "Lest perhaps the people change their minds when they see war, and return to Egypt." So* **God led the people around by way of the wilderness of the Red Sea.**

> *And the children of Israel went up in orderly ranks out of the land of Egypt.'*
>
> EXODUS 13:17-18 (NKJV)

Here we see that although the children of Israel departed Egypt equipped for battle, God led them to their destiny the longer way simply because their shoulders were not developed enough to handle the difficult battles that awaited them in the wilderness of Shur. As a result, God led them through the wilderness of Etham where there were fewer battles, and even then, they could barely deal with these small challenges as we see in Exodus 15:23-25,

> *Now when they came to Marah, they could not drink the waters of Marah, for they were bitter. Therefore the name of it was called Marah. And* **the people complained against Moses, saying, "What shall we drink?"** *So he cried out to the Lord, and the Lord showed him a tree. When he cast it into the waters, the waters were made sweet.*
>
> (NKJV)

Here, the people's murmuring was an indication that they lacked faith and the mandatory sense of godly responsibility, despite being dressed for battle upon leaving Egypt. They maintained a defeatist mindset enroute. Today it is surprising to see that believers throughout body of Christ in churches everywhere who are operating under the powerful unctions of the prophetic, the pastoral, the apostolic, the teaching, the evangelistic, and the deliverance ministries still choose to journey in their day to day Christian lives with a defeatist mentality. This attitude makes us look like orphans even though we are a royal priesthood and a holy nation. We are princes and princesses. The name of the Lord is our strong tower. It is the place that provides our shield of protection from the enemy.

Although the wilderness of Etham was the path of less resistance, it ended up prolonging the journey to the promised land—Destiny. Whenever you find yourself at the crossroad of "*Etham*" and "*Shur*", always choose *Shur*. For the path of least resistance (*Etham*) will always lead you to '*Marah', that is, bitter* waters which will cause you to grumble. The grumbling then causes God to give temporal solutions to your challenges, instead of graduating you to the next level of your destiny. Even though the path of *Shur* may be fraught with many difficulties, the one thing that we can be sure of is that, '*faithful is He who called us, Who also will do it*' (1 Thessalonians 5:24). As with the children of Israel, remember that our God has adequately clothed us with the requisite equipment to walk into our destinies. We do this by trusting in His divine provision that He brings our way day by day. This was the path David took according to Psalm 23:4.

HAVING DOMINION OVER VEILS

An understanding of the background regarding the events that took place on Mount Moriah, which resulted in the separation of father and son, is important when we look closely at the contrasting world views Isaac was confronted with, followed by how he proceeded to navigate around them.

When God instructed mankind to have dominion over the creation He spoke into existence, according to Genesis 1:26, He did in no way intend us to have dominion over one another, but rather intended us to dominate His natural creation. After Adam's fall in Genesis chapter three, however, man lost this dominion to the devil. The good news is that the second Adam (Christ Jesus) gave humanity back the dominion and authority the first Adam lost. The purpose of this redemptive dominion is to keep Satan where he belongs, under our feet, as we see in the following scripture,

> And [Jesus] said to them, "I saw **Satan fall like lightning from heaven**. Behold, I give you the **authority to trample on serpents and scorpions, and over all the power of the enemy**, and nothing shall by any means hurt you.
>
> LUKE 10:19 (NKJV)

Satan is a cunning entity. His advances toward us are highly strategic. He often comes under the cover of veils (2 Corinthians 11:14–15). It is therefore very important that we maintain spiritual sensitivity to veils from the camp of Satan.

The veil you fail to unveil today may became the troubles you have to live with tomorrow.

His ultimate aim is to derail us from the path of destiny. He *'comes to steal, to kill, and to destroy, but Jesus comes to give us life in abundance'* according to John 10:10. Satan is a master of camouflaging mega problems with sparkly wrapping. Our God, on the other hand, is a master of concealing precious treasures in unattractive wrapping. We need to be paying close attention to the appearance of stuff in our lives. It takes a spiritually alert eye to see through packaging.

The narrative in Genesis 25:5–6 informs us that before Abraham died, '… *[he]* **gave all that he had to Isaac***. But to the sons of his concubines (Hagar and Keturah), Abraham gave gifts* … (AMP). In this way, Abraham passed on 'The Blessing', the anointing that brings blessing, to Isaac and gave physical possessions to his other sons. There is a big difference between having physical possessions and possessing the thing that creates physical possessions.

Whilst the writer of the book of Genesis did not name the exact gifts that were handed out by Abraham, the thing that is certain is that Isaac received a better inheritance from his father Abraham than his brothers did. Furthermore, when considering this reality in the light of 'to whom much is given much is expected', one can naturally assume that Isaac should have been a man of deep spiritual insight. The inherent insights intended for Issac's appropriation, would have provided him with the spiritual illumination that would have in turn enabled him to see through every kind of veil that 'The Promise' he inherited attracted. But this was not the case, as we will see here.

The question of why this supposedly rich and blessed man of God would allow the stronghold of veils to cloud his spiritual conscience to the extent that he even took a woman he was not yet familiar with into his mother's tent (Genesis 24:67), remains. At least, wouldn't it have been better to take the woman into his father's tent, especially given that this option was available to him?

In the Old Testament, the word *tent* represents worship, tabernacle, or dwelling. A tabernacle, a place of worship, or a dwelling place, always has inherent rules and principles that apply to those who enter. These guiding principles or rules represent mindsets or world views.

There were basically two world views at play when Isaac absconded after the events at Mount Moriah. The first world view is what I refer to as the Abraham mind-set. This world view is that of responsibility. That is, opting for navigating experiences efficiently, which is often the most challenging option, to get the initial part of the journey over and done with. This is the quickest way to arrive at 'destiny'. The other worldview is the Sarah mindset. This view always seeks to cut corners by avoiding the tough, but otherwise correct, choices. The Bible says that,

> **Abraham stretched out his hand and took the knife to slay his son.** *But the Angel of the LORD called to him from heaven and said "Abraham, Abraham!" So he said, "Here I am." And He said,* **"Do not lay your hand on the lad, or do anything to him;** *for now I know that you* **fear God**, *since you have not withheld your son, your only son, from me."*
>
> GENESIS 22:10–12 (NKJV)

The Abrahamic world view is illustrated in this scripture. Abraham acted on the voice of God in faith without hesitation. To operate in this worldview is to align one's actions with the dictates of the divine agenda. Remember that the divine agenda can sometimes require us to go against our own feelings or fleshly desires. This scenario portrays Abraham as being somewhat mean. He did attempt to kill the son he loved, the gift God gave him. Yet, I believe he only did this because he loved God more than everything else in his life, even more than his son. This is the mindset of godly responsibility. I believe this was the mindset he was trying to teach his son Isaac.

The world view of Sarah is evident in her reaction to Isaac's return from Moriah. While it is unclear where Isaac went from Moriah, I am inclined to believe that he went to his mother. The question is, however, as a responsible mother, why did Sarah not rebuke her son for failing to learn the lessons of responsibility from a responsible father? The answer to this question is evident in the inference in Genesis 24:67, and we can rightly assume that by subscribing to his mother's world view (Genesis 22:19, 23:1–2) Isaac caused the separation from his father. No wonder Isaac could not see through veils.

> *And Isaac went out to meditate in the field in the evening; and he lifted his eyes and looked, and there, the camels were coming. Then Rebekah lifted her eyes, and when she saw Isaac she dismounted from her camel; for she had said to the servant, "Who is this man walking in the field to meet us?" The servant said, "It is my master." So **she took a veil and covered herself**. And the servant told Isaac all the things that he had done.*
>
> GENESIS 24:63–66 (NKJV)

Put simply, it is not enough to be anointed, to be gifted, to be blessed, to have an anointed spiritual or physical father, or to even be prophesied an awesome destiny. Spiritual alertness must characterise our lives, otherwise we can be rendered vulnerable and subsequently become easy targets for the enemy to enter into and to manipulate in much the same way we see him do in Genesis 24:63.

Let's try to understand revelations and seeing beyond veils. While I'm not suggesting that Rebekah is an agent of Satan here, it is obvious that Isaac was not spiritually alert enough to see beyond Rebekah's veil. What surprises me most is that Isaac was out in the field meditating when he saw his bride-to-be coming. At what point did he lose his spiritual sight? Was it a result of over excitement? Notice that while he was losing his spiritual sensitivity, probably due to a state of euphoria, Rebekah was preparing the ground by putting on a veil, in order to meet a man that she was not familiar with. Isn't it surprising that even as prayerful and spiritual believers, sometimes we can inadvertently drop our guard during the smaller breakthroughs, giving access to the enemy to harm us.

Rebekah's veil limited Isaac's sense of spiritual judgement. No wonder Isaac's life was prone to manipulation by Rebekah in many instances. Rebekah's veil, which Isaac did not deal with at the outset, maintained a state of blindness to these manipulations throughout his life. We need to be particularly careful of the kinds of people we allow entry into our innermost perimeters without first unveiling them. Interestingly, Rebekah was the sister of Laban, the man who would later take advantage of his own nephew and son-in-law Jacob.

EXPLORE YOUR SHECHEM TO THE FULLEST

We are told that Isaac married when he was forty years old (Genesis 25:20). Whilst it is acceptable in Hebrew custom for parents to play a role in choosing marriage partners for their sons, particularly in the days of Isaac, the level of parental involvement in Isaac's case was very unusual. In Genesis 24:1–4, we encounter a situation where Isaac became a candidate for marriage without first possessing the requisite tools. In particular, that of godly responsibility,

> *Now Abraham was old, well advanced in years, and the Lord had blessed Abraham in all things. And Abraham said to the eldest servant of his house [Eliezer*

> *of Damascus], who ruled over all that he had, I beg of you, put your hand under my thigh; And you shall swear by the Lord, the God of heaven and earth, that you will not take a wife for my son from the daughters of the Canaanites, among whom I have settled, But you shall go to my country and to my relatives and take a wife for my son Isaac.*
>
> GENESIS 24:1–4 (AMP)

The following questions come to mind when we reflect on this scripture: Why was Eliezer of Damascus referred to as the ruler of Abraham's house instead of Isaac? I thought Abraham asked God for a son because he understood that he would need a son not only to inherit when he died (Genesis 15:2), but to be ruler of his house while he was still alive. It is surprising that Eliezer was still being referred to as master of Abraham's house in the presence of Isaac who was a fully grown man. This is an indictment on Isaac's sense of responsibility. In spite of dwelling in an environment of responsibility in Shechem, he displayed symptoms of spiritual immaturity. Could this ineptitude on the part of Isaac be a direct result of being raised as a son rather than as a servant? Or was it his elitist upbringing that limited his ability to carry burdens? We are told that both Eliezer and Isaac were born in Abraham's house and were raised by Abraham. The only possible difference between these two men would have been the fact that one was raised as a servant and the other as a son.

Why did the responsibility of choosing a wife for Isaac not rest with Isaac himself but Eliezer of Damascus? Obviously, when a wilderness or Shechem opportunity comes our way and we do not welcome it, we allow that opportunity to be passed on to other candidates who avail themselves. No wonder Abraham had to plead with Eliezer of Damascus to swear to him that he will not take a Canaanite woman as wife for his son Isaac (Gen. 24:3). This was an indictment on Isaac's sense of judgement. Simply put, Abraham did not trust that Isaac could choose a good woman for a wife on his own. Whenever we avoid responsibility, we set in motion the injustice King Solomon described as *'servants riding horses while princes walk like servants on foot'* in Ecclesiastes 10:7, to become our portion.

Why was Eliezer of Damascus given the responsibility of searching for a wife for Isaac? In the first chapter of this book, we saw how Kish sent his son Saul to lead a search mission for his lost donkeys. Saul was the one who led the mission and not the servant. This is a clear demonstration of confidence in a responsible son. We saw a similar demonstration of confidence through Jesse when he sent his son David to take food to his older brothers who were on the battlefield (1 Samuel 17:17). Jacob also showed similar confidence by sending his son Joseph to take supplies to his older brothers in Shechem instead of relying on the services of servants.

Isaac's inaction cast doubt on his ability to shoulder his own responsibility, let alone that of others. The most surprising aspect of this narrative is in the fact that prior to meeting Rebekah, Isaac was dwelling within the wilderness, an environment of responsibility in Shechem or Canaan, right up until the moment he married her, yet he failed to allow the positive environmental influences to dominate his actions. Simply put, Isaac did not dynamically explore the wilderness environment he was living in.

A thorough exploration of a wilderness environment called Shechem is the thing that enables us to build a hedge of protection against the enemy who always comes under the cover of veils. The enemy usually comes into our lives through people who are dear to us in order to take advantage of us. Our moment in the wilderness is a time to stay alive in the daily battles Satan engages us in. It is often said that *'the serpent we tolerate in the book of Genesis grows to become the dragon in the book of Revelation'*. Wilderness situations are not meant to destroy us but rather to prepare us for advancement.

5

A SUPPLANTING SPIRIT WILL PROLONG YOUR WALK TO DESTINY: JACOB'S ADVENTURE

Having prepared our minds to understand how an inept response to spiritual prompting can cost us dearly in our journey to destiny, we can now better understand the complexity of another spiritual entity which I will refer to in this chapter as the '*supplanting spirit*'. This spirit is the '*excess baggage*' we need to off-load if we want to finish the race of our destiny by the appointed time. In the narrative rendered in Hebrews 12:1-3, the Apostle Paul gives two very good reasons why we need to concentrate on the race set before us with vigor. I want to parallel Apostle Paul's narrative here to the crux of this chapter for two reasons.

First, as the Apostle Paul indicates, due to the great cloud of witnesses cheering us on, we cannot afford to run the race in the manner we might naturally be inclined. There is too much at stake. The cloud of witnesses Paul talks about can be the many people our divine destiny is ordained to impart to. We must understand that our destinies are interwoven and the manner in which we run our race directly affects other destinies.

Second, we have an example to follow in this race. That of Jesus Christ the author and finisher of our faith. When we focus on His example, 'who for the joy set before Him was able to endure the cross', we are inspired and empowered with the necessary grace to stay on the path of righteousness on our journey to destiny.

In this chapter, we will further develop our understanding of the price of surrender to a supplanting spirit during the process of achieving excellence. We will focus on the life of yet another of the scripture's great patriarchs, Jacob also called Israel, and his struggles.

TWISTING THE ARM OF GOD

In order for us to fully understand the original intent of God when He answered Isaac's prayer regarding Rebekah's barrenness, we need to go back to the revelation Rebekah received from the Lord:

> … *and Isaac prayed much to the Lord for his wife because she was unable to bear children; and the Lord granted his prayer, and Rebekah his wife became pregnant. [Two] children struggled together within her; and she said, if it is so [that the Lord has heard our prayer], why am I like this?* **and she went to inquire of the Lord.** *The Lord said to her, [The founders of] two nations are in your womb, and the separation of two peoples has*

begun in your body; the one people shall be stronger than the other, and **the elder shall serve the younger.**

GENESIS 25:21-23 (AMP)

The amplified translation's rendering of this scripture is very succinct. We notice here that Isaac identified a problem and interceded for a solution. God decided to grant Isaac his request, but in so doing wrapped His answer with another problem. I believe that God decided to wrap the solution to the couple's problem with what appeared to Rebekah in the physical, as another problem, namely the struggle in her womb, because He wanted Rebekah to seek His presence on the matter privately. Rebekah responded accordingly, and God revealed a mystery to her, which was God's original intent regarding the destiny of the two boys.

Given that this scripture reveals that the intercession was actually done by Isaac, one must ask, why the revelation of this mystery was given solelyto Rebekah and not to both to Rebekah and Isaac? Could it be that although Isaac carried the seed of the prophetic destinies of both boys in him, God could not trust Isaac's ability to overcome his carnal desires (Genesis 25:28) in order to fulfill God's divine agenda (Genesis 25:23) as it turned out (Genesis 27:2-4)? Or could it be that even though it was Rebekah who received the revelation from God, she did not want her husband Isaac to corrupt God's agenda due to her doubts about Isaac's grounding in spiritual matters? Could this have been the reason for intercepting Isaac's plan with her alternative plan?

Either way, both plans were corrupted versions of God's original intent, and both ended up prolonging Jacob's journey to his destiny. Rebekah's action (Genesis 27:5-10) was most probably based on her personal convictions and the faith she had in the revelation she'd received from God rather than anything else. She probably thought that regardless of the method she used to execute her plan, the end was always going to justify it. Indeed, with the benefit of hindsight, we see that both plans ended up dislocating Jacob from his prophetic destiny. Rebekah's plan forced him out of Beersheba, the place in which he was actually heading in the direction of his destiny, to the strange lands of Haran (Genesis 27:42–43, 28:1). These were the lands God had instructed his grandfather Abraham to move away from, no less (Genesis 12:1–4).

Whilst these arguments appear to suggest that Jacob's predicament was inflicted on him by his parents, a careful examination of the chronology of other events relating to his subversive action, actually places the ultimate responsibility of consequences on Jacob himself. Biblical accounts estimate that Jacob was already in his early seventies when he fled to Haran. He was old enough to have taken charge of his own life in much the same way his son Joseph did prior to being sold into slavery. Jacob shouldn't have allowed his parents to derail him from his walk into destiny.

The buck of Godly responsibility stops with us, and not with others. We have to learn to take responsibility.

I have seen this happen to many people within the body of Christ time and time again in my twenty years of ministry. I have witnessed siblings, parents, friends, church elders, deacons, and even pastors and spiritual parents, who are held in high regard by younger believers in the faith, make mistakes that have caused them to backslide in the faith.

While there are instances where some of these people cite justifiable reasons for opting out, a stern word of caution is warranted here. Regardless of the justification, nothing can justify the backsliding of a believer or the giving up of the precious faith he or she has vested in our Lord Jesus Christ. Such irresponsible choices prolong the journey to one's ordained destiny and must be avoided at all cost.

A REVERSE WALK

The Bible states that Jacob was entreated by his parents to leave Beersheba and move to Haran to live with his uncle Laban after the fall out with his brother Esau. It is such a tragedy to see so many believers who find themselves in Jacob's situation today. They are often compelled by difficult circumstances in life to move from the place where the spirit of God abounds around them, to places where carnality is the order of the day. This is a reverse walk and is commonly referred to as backsliding. In Genesis 21:22–24 we see that it was in the city of Beersheba that Jacob's grandfather Abraham reached an agreement with Abimelech the King of Philistine for the return of Abraham's well,

> *And it came to pass at that time that Abimelech and Phichol, the commander of his army, spoke to Abraham, saying,* **"God is with you in all that you do.** *Now therefore, swear to me by God that you will not deal falsely with me, with my offspring, or with my posterity; but that according to the kindness that I have done to you, you will do to me and to the land in which you have dwelt."* **And Abraham said, "I will swear."**
>
> (NKJV)

Then when we move one generation forward, we see a similar agreement between the same Abimelech and Jacob's father Isaac in the same city of Beersheba,

> *Then Abimelech came to [Isaac] from Gerar, with Ahuzzath one of his friends, and Phichol the commander of his army. And Isaac said to them, "Why have you come to me, since you hate me and have sent me away from you?" But they said,* **"We have certainly seen that the LORD is with you. So we said, "Let there now be an oath between us, between you and us; and let us make a covenant with you, that you wilt do us no harm,** *since we have not touched you, and since we have done nothing to you but good, and have sent you away in peace. You are now the blessed of the LORD".*
>
> GENESIS 26:26–29 (NKJV)

Here, we see that it was Abimelech who made the move toward Isaac and not the other way around. Abimilech had observed a strange thing happening to Isaac when he was an enemy back in Beersheba. This strange thing was so glorious that Abimelech could not restrain himself from reaching out. I can imagine the highly conspicuous, phenomenal, and powerful anointing that was on Isaac, an anointing so obvious that it even attracted the attention of a King of Abimelech's caliber. Even though the level of mistrust and enmity between the two men would have been such that very few would have expected King Abimelech to humble himself in the way that he did by submitting to Isaac, the king was compelled.

Regardless of the animosity, it was King Abimelech who took the initiative to make contact. This is the kind of favour God clothes us with once we decide to follow His guidance. The secret of the divine favour that was so evident in the life

A Supplanting Spirit will Prolong Your Walk to Destiny

of Isaac had to do with dwelling in a location called Gerar where God's presence was (Genesis 26:23-25). This divine presence was only specific to Isaac. The identification of this location based on the voice of God was the thing that set Isaac apart.

Note here that if a heathen like Abimelech could sense the presence of the Lord in Beersheba, compelling him to go to great lengths to reach out and partake of the anointing that was on Isaac, an anointing that had been made visible by God's glory, then it naturally follows that we would have expected much more from Jacob. Jacob should have allowed his spiritual senses to prompt him not to depart from Beersheba. Jacob should have known, even more so than Abimelech had before him, the value of the covenant he had with God. He should have known the importance of dwelling in God's presence and not to trade it under any circumstances.

As discussed in chapter three, we know that one of the reasons Terah moved his family from Ur was because of the pain caused by the death of his son Haran, Abraham's brother.

**It takes effort to make every step but not every step takes you to the right place.
Play it smart by relying on divine insights.**

Given this background, one would have expected Jacob to avoid making the same mistake given the awareness of his family's history and the consequences associated with their unsolicited move. Yet, even knowledge of the predicament his ancestors found themselves in, in the city of Haran could not deter him. Remember it was in this city that the Terah family separated. Nahor and the rest of Haran's family were left behind after Abraham's exodus, according to Genesis 12:1.

There are two questions that naturally follow here. First, why would Jacob allow himself to be forced into taking refuge in Haran, especially given his knowledge of the history? Second, why would Jacob take cover under the roof of the extremely carnal character that was his uncle Laban, given that he knew the family's history with him?

I am convinced that Jacob was in possession of all the facts, particularly given that he was already in his seventies at the time he fled his home in Beersheba. Sadly, Jacob's decision is a clear case of spiritual irresponsibility, which inevitably and ultimately prolonged his journey to destiny. The entire period he spent in Haran with his uncle Laban was wasted time. The fact that he was aware of this is confirmed in his allusion to his regret in his response to Pharaoh's question when he was in Egypt.

> 'Pharaoh said to Jacob, "How old are you?" And Jacob said to Pharaoh, "The days of the years of my pilgrimage are one hundred and thirty years; few and evil have been the days of the years of my life, and they have not attained to the days of the years of the life of my fathers in the days of their pilgrimage".'
>
> GENESIS 47:8–9 (NKJV)

A background check of the man Laban will inform us that he was a descendant of Nahor, the brother of Abraham. When God instructed Abraham to leave his family and kindred and move to a place He would show him (Genesis 12:1), He was referring to Nahor, the brother of Abraham, his children, and those of Haran. I believe that the reason God instructed Abraham to leave these people behind, because the mindset they possessed was contrary to what was required to fulfill the plans God had for Abraham.

CROSSING THE JORDAN IS NOT ENOUGH

While preparing to return to Canaan, Jacob made a profound statement in Genesis 32:9-10, that I want to have a closer look at here,

> *And Jacob said, O God of my father Abraham, and God of my father Isaac, the Lord which said unto me, Return unto thy country, and to thy kindred, and I will deal well with thee:* **I am not worthy of the least of all the mercies, and of all the truth, which thou hast shewed unto thy servant; for with my staff I passed over this Jordan; and now I am become two bands.**
>
> GENESIS 32:9-10 (NKJV)

This statement is loaded with mysteries related to Jacob's rediscovery of the path to his divine destiny. In this scripture Jacob attributes his material prosperity whilst working for his uncle Laban in Haran, to the mercies of God. He did not attribute it to his human ability, contrary to the impression that is often derived from Genesis 30:31-32. Jacob also makes a distinction between the first time he crossed the Jordan on his way to Haran as a fugitive, and the second time when he crossed the Jordan as a wealthy man. He clarifies that when he crossed the Jordan the first time it was with personal belongings representing the blessing he received from Isaac his father. He also emphasises that he had since increased both materially and relationally indeed, by the time he embarked on his second crossing of the Jordan.

Jacob's emphasis on material increase suggests that he had already fulfilled divine destiny in part by earthly means via personal accomplishments. Contrary to this thinking at the time, however, although he was wealthy by all standards, Jacob was still living outside the mandated territory of his divine destiny. Isn't it amazing that so many people labour to achieve material prosperity as a direct result of maintaining a mindset that dictates that material acquisition and worldly achievements alone will enable the fulfillment of destiny? We see Jacob give a glowing tribute to his God in this scripture only to turn back in the next verse and express the depths of fear he was still living in,

> *Deliver me, I pray, from the hand of my brother, from the hand of Esau; **for I fear him**, lest he come and attack me and the mother with the children.*
>
> GENESIS 32:11 (NKJV)

In spite of all his accomplishments, Jacob was still intimidated by his brother Esau's success (Genesis 32:3–7). Jacob was so overwhelmed that he could not even trust God who he had encountered at Peniel and who had instructed him to return to Canaan (Genesis 31:3) where He promised Jacob that he would be protected from his brother Esau's wrath.

A fulfilled destiny is one reached on God's terms, by his guidance, at a specific location He predestined.

A Supplanting Spirit will Prolong Your Walk to Destiny

Although Jacob was prosperous, he still had the mindset of a fugitive. His first encounter at the Jordan could not deliver him from this mentality. He needed a second encounter.

It took divine intervention for the yoke of fear that dominated Jacob's life to be broken once and for all. Let's see how Jacob's second journey to the Jordan, also known as Jabbok River—tributary of the Jordan, actually played out and what he gained from that encounter. The Bible says that,

> *'[Jacob] arose that night and took his two wives, his two female servants, and his eleven sons, and passed over the ford Jabbok. He took them, sent them over the brook, and sent over what he had.* ***Then Jacob was left alone;*** *and then a Man wrestled with him* ***until the breaking of day.*** *Now when He saw that He did not prevail against him,* ***He touched the socket of his hip;*** *and the socket of Jacob's hip was out of joint as He wrestled with him. And He said, "Let me go, for the day breaks". But he said, "I will not let You go, unless You bless me!". So He said to him, "What is your name?" He said, "Jacob". And He said, "Your name shall no longer be called Jacob, but Israel;* ***for you have struggled with God and with men, and have prevailed."*** *Then Jacob said, "Tell me Your name, I pray." And He said, "Why is it that you ask about My name?" And he blessed him there.* ***And Jacob called the name of the place Peniel: "For I have seen God face to face, and my life is preserved."***
>
> GENESIS 32:22-30 (NKJV)

Notice a strange thing happening here. In Genesis 32:10, we see Jacob flaunting his credentials as an achiever. His posture in this scripture suggests to me that his material possessions were his main source of happiness at this point in his life. I can imagine that it would have been a big sacrifice for him to part company with his material possessions and family relationships, in the manner in which he did in Genesis 32:22–23. I wonder what would have prompted him to take this action. Nevertheless, he did, and notice what happened when he took that bold step of selfdenial, a denial of his fleshly desires. I can imagine the effort it would have taken to shut the door to the convenience that he had become so accustomed to. I am talking about the decision to take his family and possessions to the other side of Jabbok.

It was only after this sacrificial act that Jacob encountered the angel of the Lord, who gave him the name Israel, his original name according to heaven's database. In the concluding episode of the encounter, Jacob made a revealing statement which I want us to ponder very soberly. He named the place Peniel because he saw God face to face. I did a background check into all of Jacob's previous encounters with God, either directly or through angels, and realised that at no other time had he seen God face to face. In all his encounters prior to arriving at Peniel, Jacob had only heard from God through dreams.

There is a big difference between hearing from God through visions and dreams, and seeing God face to face. In the Old Testament dispensation, only spiritual men such as Abraham, Moses, Joshua, Gideon, and Manoa—to name a few—saw God face to face. Almost all these divine visitations took place whilst God was in the process of transmitting information to these individuals in order to execute His divine agenda here on earth. The encounter with the Angel of the Lord at Jabbok redirected Jacob into the original destiny that God had planned for him from his mother's womb (Genesis 25:23). In Genesis 32:30, Jacob commented on how his life had been preserved after his encounter with God.

A Supplanting Spirit will Prolong Your Walk to Destiny

There are some valuable lessons we can learn from Jacob's encounter at Jabbok. Jacob did not prayerfully request angelic visitations, neither did any of his relatives or friends make such prayer requests on his behalf. The Lord decided to appear when Jacob was alone, after having parted company with everything that he valued, namely his material possessions and family relationships. We learn that sacrifice attracts divine visitations.

In addition to this, the angel of the Lord did not appear to Jacob in peace as would have been expected. The scripture says that the angel wrestled with him. It was my grandfather in the Lord, the Archbishop Nicholas Duncan Williams who said, *"The world does not give you what you deserve, it gives you what you fight for"*. Here the angel of the Lord chose to come at night rather than during the day. This was the moment when Jacob would have been most vulnerable due to weariness and weakness. The Apostle Paul makes a similar point when he says that as Christians, we must crucify our fleshly desires,

> *"And those who are Christ's have crucified the flesh with its passions and desires. If we live in the Spirit, let us also walk in the Spirit."*
>
> GALATIANS 5:24-25 (NKJV)

The travails Jacob encountered at the brook of Jabbok on that night tested his sense of godly responsibility. He did not run away from the angel of the Lord. He endured until he prevailed over the angel. No wonder he left the brook of Jabbok with a limp on his way to reuniting with his family. This was the scar in his life that gave him the name *Israel*, exulting him to the status of one of the patriarchs of our Christian faith.

In the book of Joshua, we see another instance where trials were endured by a group of people for the purpose of the rediscovery of their destinies. Joshua, the son of Nun made a profound statement when he was leading the children of Israel across the Jordan river to Jericho.

> 'So Joshua said to the children of Israel, "Come here, and hear the words of the LORD your God". And Joshua said, "By this you shall know that the living God is among you, and that He will without fail drive out from before you the Canaanites and the Hittites and the Hivites, and the Perizzites, and the Girgashites, and the Amorites, and the Jebusites. Behold, the ark of the covenant of the Lord of all the earth is crossing over before you into Jordan'.
>
> JOSHUA 3:9–11 (NKJV)

Here we see that God informs His people of the earthly accomplishments He had prepared for them on the other side of the Jordan. But the story does not end there. God made that promise in order to keep their hopes alive so that they would endure the battles ahead of them.

God then went a step further to reveal to them the nature of those necessary trials and difficulties. He knew the importance of these challenges in the process of preparing them to be responsible. Trials help us become responsible. It is only after we become responsible that we are able to execute our divine purpose here on earth according to heaven's terms. In order for the children of Israel to sustain the gains associated with the blessings that were ahead of them in Canaan (Joshua 3:9–11), God needed to teach them *godly responsibility*. This kind of responsibility comes by the lifting of burdens as we see in the following scripture,

A Supplanting Spirit will Prolong Your Walk to Destiny

And it came to pass, when all the people had completely crossed over the Jordan, that the Lord spoke to Joshua, saying, "Take for yourselves twelve men from the people, one man from every tribe, and command them, saying, **'Take for yourselves twelve stones from here, out of the midst of the Jordan,** *from the place where the priests' feet stood firm. You shall carry them over with you and leave them in the lodging place where you lodge tonight."' Then* **Joshua called the twelve men** *whom he had appointed from the children of Israel, one man from every tribe; and Joshua said to them: "Cross over before the ark of the Lord your God into the midst of the Jordan, and* **each one of you take up a stone on his shoulder,** *according to the number of the tribes of the children of Israel, that this may be a sign among you when your children ask in time to come, saying, 'What do these stones mean to you?' Then you shall answer them that the waters of the Jordan were cut off before the ark of the covenant of the Lord; when it crossed over the Jordan, the waters of the Jordan were cut off.* **And these stones shall be for a memorial to the children of Israel forever."**

JOSHUA 4:1-7 (NKJV)

We see a repeat of Jacob's encounter at the brook of Jabbok where he had to leave his family and possessions on the other side of the river to fight for his destiny. The problem with many believers is that they want to rediscover their God-given destiny but are unwilling to pay the price of sacrifice.

Furthermore, we see that the children of Israel had already crossed the Jordan river but they hadn't done so with a sacrifice. They needed to have a sacrificial encounter in order to open the windows of the heavens over their divine destiny that was Canaan. We see Joshua offer this sacrifice by returning to the Jordan river with selected men in order to engage in a wrestling match. Notice the type of wrestling match the men were asked to engage in. They were instructed to *take up stones onto their shoulders*. Here the men left the ark, which represented the promise, with the multitude on the other side of Jordan in order to pursue godly responsibility by lifting stones from the bed of the river onto their shoulders. It takes the vital ingredient of sacrifice and of godly responsibility to fulfil the promises of God in our lives.

The final question arising from this text is why didn't God ask the people to pick up stones from the bank of the river. This would have been easier. He asked them to to pick up stones from the depths of the river bed which was very difficult by comparison. More often than not our walk with God is punctuated with trials for the fulfillment of His purpose. As believers in these last days, instead of praying for trial-free lives, we should be praying for the grace to overcome when God allows all manner of trials to intercept us.

We see a similar occurrence when Elijah and Elisha were crossing the same Jordan river in 2 Kings 2:9–10,

> *And so it was, when they had crossed over, that Elijah said to Elisha, "Ask! What may I do for you, before I am taken away from you?" Elisha said, "Please let a double portion of your spirit be upon me." So he said, "You have asked a hard thing. Nevertheless,* **if you see me when I am taken from you***, it shall be so for you; but if not, it shall not be so".*
>
> (NKJV)

Here, both men crossed the Jordan and a promise was made to Elisha, albeit accompanied by a condition. In the following verse we see that after the condition was met on his return home Elisha had to cross the Jordan river again. However, he needed to make the waters part so he could cross this time. In 2 Kings 2:11-13 we see that Elisha took his departed master's coat and struck the waters before crossing,

> *Then it happened, as they continued on and talked, that suddenly a chariot of fire appeared with horses of fire, and separated the two of them; and Elijah went up by a whirlwind into heaven.* **And Elisha saw it, and he cried out,** *"My father, my father, the chariot of Israel and its horsemen!" So he saw him no more. And* **he took hold of his own clothes and tore them into two pieces. He also took up the mantle of Elijah that had fallen from him,** *and went back and stood by the bank of the Jordan.*
>
> (NKJV)

You will notice that the vital ingredient which activated Elijah's prophetic mantle on his servant Elisha surprisingly wasn't Elijah's coat. The secret to the activation of the prophetic mantle on Elisha's life was the series of trials and difficulties he had to endure throughout their journey from Gilgal up until crossing the Jordan the second time (2 Kings 2:2,4,6). However, the pivotal act that ultimately lifted Elisha from a mere servant of a prophet to ascending into his prophetic destiny was the point when he cried and tore his clothes after realising that his master was taken away from him (2 Kings 2:12).

He had proven beyond reasonable doubt to his God, that the motivation for his desire for his master's mantle was not a desire to possess the power of the prophetic anointing upon his life, but rather his love for God. I believe his tears were a demonstration of his sadness for the cessation of the good works God was doing through the life of his master the prophet Elijah.

6

OVERCOMING THE SELF: JOSEPH'S BROTHERS

Jacob's son's awareness of the price he had paid during his subversion, should have naturally predisposed them to being responsible with the things related to the purposes of the God their father had encountered at Peniel. However, this was not the case. The snare of impunity overcame the house of Israel. This outcome had been motivated by selfish and lustful desires. This stronghold ended up destroying the destinies of sons who were ordained as kings and priests by virtue of blood connection to the promise God made to their ancestor Abraham. They instead ended up dying as ordinary men in Egypt. It took the anointing on the life of Joseph, the eleventh son, to break this yoke of impunity. Joseph's sense of godly responsibility distinguished him from his siblings. The adversities he confronted in Shechem and Egypt prepared him for that spectacular destiny.

Here, we will only look closely at the first four sons of Israel: Reuben, Simeon, Levi, and Judah. The Hebrew custom at the time, and which I believe still applies today, was that the sons Israel had with his concubines were not heirs to his inheritance. This reality places Joseph next in line after Leah's sons, even though he was the eleventh son.

Scripture tells us that Zebulun and Issachar, the last two sons of Leah, were born after Leah bribed Rachel with Reuben's mandrakes prior to getting access to Jacob's bed (Genesis 30:15–17). These two sons, therefore, were procured on the altar of Leah's jealousy by virtue of Reuben's mandrakes. Spiritually, these two sons became subject to Joseph, even though they were older than Joseph in the physical sense.

The focus here will be on the specific actions of the first four sons that gave Satan the opportunity to truncate their destinies vis-a-vis the exemplary life of Joseph.

CONTROL YOUR LUSTFUL DESIRES

As the first son of Jacob, it was Reuben's birthright to be a son of power and might, as is evidenced in this scripture,

> *"Reuben, you are my firstborn, My might and the beginning of my strength, The excellency of dignity and the excellency of power. Unstable as water, you shall not excel, Because you went up to your father's bed; Then you defiled it—He went up to my couch.*
>
> GENESIS 49:3–4 (NKJV)

The first thing we see here is the prophetic dimension from which Israel was making these declarations. We see that it was no longer the carnal Jacob talking, but the spiritual man Israel, after he had seen God face to face at the brook of Jabbok. We see that Reuben started off in life as 'the excellency of Israel's strength', and a child full of potential, but ended up dying as a common man in Egypt without a legacy like his younger brother's.

This scripture reiterates the fact that although God can have wonderful plans for every one of us (Jeremiah 29:11), the path we decide to take in life either takes us to His prescribed destination or a destination that will be prescribed to us by Satan the enemy. It is obvious that Reuben decided to take a strange path which led him to a destiny of instability and ultimately robbed him of the excellent spirit intended by God to guide him into his divine destiny, much like God later guided Joseph, his younger brother, in chapter two.

This invariably evokes some tough questions. For one, how can the mere defilement of a father's bed inflict such irreversible consequences on the life of a son? In other words, how could Israel be so unforgiving in pronouncing such a curse on the son he had referred to as *'the excellency of his strength'*?

We need to closely examine scripture in order to understand the circumstances that caused Reuben to commit this abomination, and to unravel the mystery surrounding Reuben's conduct. Especially that it ultimately caused him to defect from the life of 'trailblazer' that he had been born to become in the house of Israel. Sadly, he remained ordinary. We read that,

> *'... so it was, as [Rachel's] soul was departing (for she died), that she called his name Ben-Oni; but his father called him Benjamin. So Rachel died and was buried on the way to Ephrath (that is, Bethlehem). And Jacob set a pillar on her grave, which is the pillar of Rachel's grave to this day. Then Israel journeyed and pitched his tent beyond the tower of Eder. And it happened, when Israel dwelt in that land, that* **Reuben went and lay**

with Bilhah his father's concubine; and Israel heard about it'.

GENESIS 35:18–22 (NKJV)

The Bible states that it was when the household of Israel was moving from Bethel, the house of God, to Bethlehem, the place of fruitfulness, that Rachel died after giving birth to Benjamin. The question is, why would Reuben choose to defile his father's bed by sleeping with Bilhah, his father's concubine, after Rachel's death? Could it be that he had this intention all along but refrained from acting on it due to Rachel's presence? Or could it be that he did not understand the significance of the time and season that his family was in? This was the time God was in the process of promoting the family from a place of dwelling in His presence to a place of fruitfulness.

What will take years of a concentrated Christian life to build can be ruined by lustful desires in a few minutes.

Reuben, the first son of Israel, demonstrated a lack of spiritual intelligence by failing to abstain from the lust of his flesh. His selfish desire clouded his sense of judgement. He did not understand the significance of the time and the season. The possession of this ability is a vital mark of the presence of godly responsibility on a leader.

The scripture reveals that these incidents happened in Migdal Eder, the place where livestock was raised for sacrifice in God's temple, but Reuben didn't get it. He did not understand that God took the family to Eder in order to prepare them for His glory. The environment at Eder was intended to remind Reuben of what God was about to do for the family. It was a time when he should have been reflecting on the loss of his stepmother Rachel and thinking about the inclusion of the newborn baby called Benjamin, the son of the right hand, and of strength. Reuben chose to do the opposite of what he was being prepared by God to do.

There is a vital related point raised by the prophet Samuel in 1 Samuel 10:1–2 while he was anointing Saul as king of Israel that I want to draw our attention to,

Then Samuel took a flask of oil and poured it on his head, and kissed him and said: "Is it not because the Lord has anointed you commander over His inheritance? When you have departed from me today, you will find two men by Rachel's tomb in the territory of Benjamin at Zelzah; and they will say to you, 'The donkeys which you went to look for have been found. And now your father has ceased caring about the donkeys and is worrying about you, saying, "What shall I do about my son?"

1 SAMUEL 10:1–2 (NKJV)

Here, the prophet Samuel was cautioning Saul about the test of leadership that Reuben had failed. As to whether Saul really understood it or not is another matter. Nevertheless, the prophet specifically told Saul that certain events were going to take place at Rachel's tomb, on his journey back home. The prophet went further by linking Rachel's tomb with two contrasting regions, that of Benjamin, a place of divine strength, and Zelzah, a place of shadows and darkness, where Saul was to encounter two men who had a message.

It is important to note that the boundary region of these two places was the location where Saul was to receive the message from the two men. I want to submit that these two places have to do with our varying world views or beliefs systems. Our world view determines the kind of messages we receive, be they godly or worldly, and the manner in which we act on such messages determines our result. The quality of a message is as good as the location, the worldview from whence the message is received. In the case of Reuben, the journey through the wilderness did not adequately clarify his world view.

This scripture states that Rachel's tomb was at Zelzah, the place of darkness. In other words, Rachel's tomb marks the crossroad where the choice between the godly way and the way of the flesh, that is carnality and darkness, has to be made. This is the spot where God sends his messengers with the good news to us, much like the two men in this scripture. As to whether we receive, believe, and act on this message is what will either take us back to Benjamin, the place of strength, or keep us in perpetual darkness. Rachel's death was the crossroad where Reuben missed the road marker on the route to his destiny due to flesh and lustful desire.

Isn't it surprising that the birthright Jacob stole from his brother Esau would be the birthright his older sons Reuben, Simeon, Levi, and Judah would take for granted? The Bible states that the birthright of the house of Israel, the house of special privilege, was originally reserved for Reuben by virtue of being Israel's first born son,

> *Now the sons of Reuben the firstborn of Israel—he was indeed the firstborn, but because he defiled his father's bed, his birthright was given to the sons of Joseph, the son of Israel, so that the genealogy is not listed according to the birthright.*
>
> 1 CHRONICLES 5:1 (NKJV)

However, after Reuben defiled his father's bed, the birthright became available to any of his brothers. Godly responsibility became the only criteria for taking on this birthright. The adversities Joseph endured from Shechem through Egypt placed him ahead of his brothers, who had had the same opportunities but failed to utilise them. Reuben's birthright was thus passed on to Joseph through Manasseh and Ephraim. No wonder these two tribes are among the most powerful tribes in Israel even till this day.

DEAL WITH YOUR TEMPER

The scriptures state that after temporarily dwelling in Bethel, Migdal Eder, Peniel, and Succoth, Israel and his family finally moved to Shechem, where they settled permanently in line with the divine agenda,

> And Jacob journeyed to Succoth, built himself a house, and made booths for his livestock. Therefore the name of the place is called Succoth. Then Jacob came safely to the city of Shechem, which is in the land of Canaan, when he came from Padan Aram; and he pitched his tent before the city. And he bought the parcel of land, where he had pitched his tent, from the children of Hamor, Shechem's father, for one hundred pieces of money. Then he erected an altar there and called it El Elohe Israel.
>
> GENESIS 33:17–20 (NKJV)

In Genesis 31:3,13, we are told that God instructed Jacob to return to the land of Canaan where his ancestors lived. However, the specifics of the return journey, that is, the trials they would encounter along the way, were not revealed at the very beginning. I believe God kept this secret from the Israel family for a good reason. God in His ultimate wisdom knew that the family needed a test that would determine their level of endurance. This was a vital ingredient in preparing them for the glory awaiting them in Canaan. It is evident here that Shechem was the place God had in mind when He gave Jacob the instruction to return.

The scripture also states that when the family arrived in Shechem, they were offered land where they camped (Genesis 33:18b). Surprisingly, it was the children of Hamor, the King of the Hivites, who did them this favour.

Given that this group of Hivites were so generous and influential in the resettlement and integration of the house of Israel in the land of Shechem, as clearly stated in scripture, it is inconceivable and difficult to understand why Simeon and Levi would commit an act of atrocity against the hand that fed them when they arrived. The main victim of this atrocity was the prince of the land of Shechem, who the Bible says: *"was the most respected man of his family"* (Genesis 34:19b).

The most surprising part of this narrative is the fact that when the prince and his father were asked to pay the price, by agreeing to be circumcised, the ultimate confirmation of acceptance, in order for everyone to live as a united people, they did so willingly (Genesis 34:14–17). The sons of Israel responded without hesitation, even though they harboured a hidden agenda. So, my question is, why would they respond to this kind gesture with such outrage?

It seems to me that, while the sons of Israel might have been asking for a mere physical expression of cleansing via circumcision, Hamor and his son Shechem were thinking more of the spiritual significance of circumcision, that is, the cleansing of their hearts in order to embrace the God of Abraham, Isaac, and Jacob. For this worthy cause, the prince of Shechem and his father Hamor gladly responded as a result of the love they had for the God of Israel (Genesis 34:20–24).

Simeon and Levi had the perfect opportunity to learn the lesson of responsibility. Their lesson of responsibility was to give to the people of Samaria, Shechem, Hamor, and his subjects. They did not understand their Shechem season and therefore missed it. This is what Jesus wanted to teach us in His encounter with the Samaritan woman in John 4:4–34.

For Simeon and Levi to turn back a couple of days later and kill the men who demonstrated such outstanding love for the God of Israel, was an act in direct contrast with the agenda of heaven. The key motivation behind this wicked act according to Genesis 34:25–26 was pain and anger.

Without a sense of godly responsibility, recklessness become inevitable.

This heinous act demonstrates that the trials God brought to the household of Israel on their return journey to Canaan were misunderstood. The trials were meant to prepare and instill the ability to shape their God-given destiny in the future that awaited them in Canaan. This was grossly abused. No wonder this action ended up truncating their destinies, as their father Israel would later confirm through the prophetic unction that,

> 'Cursed be their anger, for it is fierce; And their wrath, for it is cruel! I will divide them in Jacob And scatter them in Israel'.
>
> GENESIS 49:7 (NKJV)

You will notice here that Israel uses the words *'division'* and *'scattering'* to characterise the consequence of evil, the consequence of the actions committed by Simeon and Levi, and the manner in which their destinies would be truncated. This is the devastation that the canker called anger can cause in our destiny when left unrestrained. There are many people within the body of Christ in a similar predicament in our day just as in years past. Even though we can make a considerable effort to reposition ourselves in order to maintain the right trajectory on the path to our God-given destiny, sadly, and much too often, we allow unrestrained anger to get the better of us.

When we take a second look at this scripture, we notice that Israel, who was in the prophetic realm, mentions names such as *'Israel'* and *'Jacob'* to define the *'physical'* and *'spiritual'* realms. In other words, Israel was prophesying to his sons Simeon and Levi that, *"I will divide your physical gifts and spiritual inheritance among your brethren."* This is similar to the distinction Abraham made between the son of his promise, Isaac, by leaving him the 'spiritual' inheritance, and only giving material gifts to his other sons (Genesis 25:5–6).

REMAIN SPIRITUALLY ALERT AT ALL TIMES

The name Judah means praise in the Hebrew language. In Genesis 29:32–35, the Bible states that Leah named her fourth son *Judah,* 'Praise' because she was frustrated by not having been shown love by Jacob in the manner that her sister Rachel had. Leah thought that after giving Jacob a third son, the playing field should have been levelled. Leah was saying in her heart that, *'God, I now put You first instead of trying to please my husband'*. In the latter part of Genesis

29:35 there is something interesting I want us to take a closer look at,

> And [Leah] conceived again and bore a son, and said, "Now I will praise the Lord." Therefore she called his name Judah. Then she stopped bearing.
> GENESIS 29:35 (NKJV)

It is easy to see Leah's decision to honour God out of a sincere and genuine experience as a contradiction. Especially given that her husband had shown lack of appreciation. She would have felt very let down by him. Notice how God responds to this demonstration of honour and gratitude. He shuts her womb. This is what happens to many people in the body of Christ today. We often do everything we can within our human capacity for this good God, and sometimes it appears that the reward we receive from Him is counterproductive to our wellbeing.

While a show of gratitude to God can initiate you into spiritual alertness, it will take godly responsibility to maintain it.

The truth about Leah's experience with God in this story was that God was making a case to both Leah and the whole of Israel's household. That as far as He was concerned, the birth of the son she had named Judah (Praise the Lord), was all that she would ever need to make her mark as a fulfilled wife and mother. This was the truth that God confirmed with the birth of Judah: *'The reward for all the effort you*

(Leah), have invested in trying to win the love of your husband Jacob, prior to turning your hopes and trust in Me Jehovah, is the gift of Judah'. It is surprising that even Leah herself did not understand the magnitude in its fullness of her praise and trust in God. Judah was the seed which produced the Messiah, Christ Jesus, and His throne which was to be established by David His servant, as prophesied by Israel,

> *The scepter shall not depart from Judah, Nor a lawgiver from between his feet, Until Shiloh comes; And to Him shall be the obedience of the people.*
>
> GENESIS 49:10 (NKJV)

As a matter of fact, the household of Israel did not need any other son to fulfil their divine destiny as a family. However, The All Knowing God that He is, foresaw that Reuben, Simeon, Levi, and Judah, would miss the mark, therefore, He allowed Rachel and Leah, and their slave girls, to bear more sons for Jacob. Judah was supposed to be the spiritual eye of the house of Israel. He was meant to be the eye that would see beyond impossibilities in the same way Joshua and Caleb had. Even after his fall, before Israel and his sons relocated to Egypt, it was Judah who was dispatched to spy out the land and to confer with his brother Joseph in preparation for their arrival (Genesis 46:28).

The fact that Judah was chosen to fulfill this assignment in the presence of three of his older brothers is a clear indication that he was intended to be the strongest of the brothers in the area of spiritual insight.

The tough question here is, why would a son with such a great destiny be carried away by ineptitude in the area of spiritual matters to such an extent that he would commit an abomination with his own daughter-in-law?

> *Now in the process of time the daughter of Shua, Judah's wife, died; and Judah was comforted, and went up to his sheep shearers at Timnah, he and his friend Hirah the Adullamite. And it was told to Tamar, saying, "Look, your father-in-law is going up to Timnah to shear his sheep."* **So she took off her widow's garments, covered herself with a veil and wrapped herself, and sat in an open place which was on the way to Timnah;** *for she saw that Shelah was grown, and she was not given to him as a wife.* **When Judah saw her, he thought she was a harlot, because she had covered her face.** *Then he turned to her by the way, and said, "Please let me come in to you"; for he did not know that she was his daughter-in-law. So she said, "What will you give me, that you may come in to me?" And he said, "I will send a young goat from the flock." So she said, "Will you give me a pledge till you send it?"*
>
> GENESIS 38:12–17 (NKJV)

I am inclined to believe that the motivation behind Judah's incestuous act was due more to a lack of spiritual alertness than to lust. I say this based on three main reasons. The writer of the book of Genesis establishes a sound context for the circumstances which led Judah to go into Timnath. The purpose for Judah's trip to Timnath, as we've read, was the business of shearing his sheep. This suggests that his action was not premeditated. It is therefore unlikely that his actions would have been motivated by lust.

The scripture states that Judah had already overcome the loss of his wife, the daughter of Shuah, at the time he committed that act. So, the issue of seeking comfort from a woman was not pressing enough to have lured him into the ditch that he eventually found himself in. Furthermore, given that we know that Tamar covered herself with a veil and sat in an open place suggests that it was Tamar who did the bidding. All that Judah should have done was to remain alert. This, he definitely failed to do.

Obviously, the ultimate responsibility of protecting the great destiny God had for Judah rested with no one else but Judah himself. The name '*Timnah*' in the Hebrew language means restraint. Although Judah's trip to this place was for business, the one thing he failed to understand was restraint of his fleshly desires. Many believers find themselves in this predicament today. With the majority of missions, mission trips, and projects we embark on, we sometimes forget the silent voice that urges us to *stay alert* to the devices of the enemy.

Remember it was in this same city of Timnah that mighty Samson gave in to the cunning manipulations of the daughter of the Philistines (Judges 14:1–18). The fact that Judah allowed the enemy to use his own daughter-in-law to truncate his destiny, adds him to the list of failures which includes Reuben, Simeon, and Levi. Spiritual ineptitude is prolonging the destinies of many believers within the body of Christ today. We have sadly taken too many things for granted.

7

THE MYSTERY BEHIND JOSEPH'S BONES

There is no doubt that Joseph left an indelible mark on the history of human civilization. Not only was he revered in the days of ancient Egypt and among his Hebrew contemporaries, but even in this present day the records of his outstanding achievements remain, and as living epistles testify of the spirit of excellence that characterised his life. Without the medium that has secured the principles that underpinned his successes, the heights achieved by this great icon of ancient Egyptian civilization would have eroded and sunk into obscurity and oblivion with the passage of time, like that of many.

In this chapter we will take a closer look at the mysteries behind Joseph's bones, and very importantly, at what message Joseph wished to portray to the unborn generations at the time of his death. He obviously foresaw that his legacy could not stand the full test of time alone. The one thing that he was certain about was that the principles on which his legacy was birthed were eternal. I believe this was why he requested his bones to be taken back to the promised land. He needed to conceal these principles of excellence for posterity.

CARRY MY BONES WITH YOU

Joseph is and will forever be a remarkable hero among the children of Israel. He was the brain behind the transformation of the ancient Egyptian economy and the structure of society. Not only did his life bring honour and dignity to his kinsmen and his entire generation, but even till this day his name is held in high esteem. He was, is, and will always be the embodiment of excellence to many generations in the body of Christ. The imprint of his life will continue to inspire many generations to come. The question is, what is the quality so unique in this man that it set him apart from others so dynamically? I believe that the answer to this question is encrypted in Genesis 50:24–25. We know that when Joseph's father Israel was about to die, he requested his corpse to be taken to Canaan for burial,

> *When the time drew near that Israel must die, he called his son Joseph and said to him, "Now if I have found favour in your sight, please put your hand under my thigh, and deal kindly and truly with me.* ***Please do not bury me in Egypt, but let me lie with my fathers; you shall carry me out of Egypt and bury me in their burial place.****" And he said, "I will do as you have said.*
>
> GENESIS 47:29–30 (NKJV)

I thought that Joseph, the one to whom this request was directed, would have wanted his body to be transported to the same place for burial after his own death. He decided to break the traditions of his fathers.

True champions leave footprints that inspire generations to come after they pass on.

He did not want to be counted among the failings of his ancestors represented by the tomb at the Cave of Machpelah (Genesis 23:1–20) after his death. He wanted to represent a new generation. The generation of outstanding achievers! The generation of excellence! Here is what this great man of God said to his brethren,

> "... I am dying; but God will surely visit you, and bring you out of this land to the land of which He swore to Abraham, to Isaac, and to Jacob." Then Joseph took an oath from the children of Israel, saying, "God will surely visit you, and **you shall carry up my bones from here.**"
> GENESIS 50:24–25 (NKJV)

Amazingly, Joseph's will differed from his father's in two ways. First, he wanted only his bones to be taken back home to Canaan, and second, he left the burial location unmentioned, demonstrating godly responsibility. I believe Joseph was making the following two statements.

That he was reserving the secrets that had underpinned his excellence for the future generations to discover, who would in turn recognise the God of Abraham, Isaac, and Jacob as their God.

That he wanted this generation of believers to know that the keys to excellence rest with accepting godly responsibility.

DIVINE KEYS TO EXCELLENCE

The Bible states that Joseph reached an agreement with the Children of Israel for his will to be transmitted to future generations of believers (Genesis 50:25). Three important questions come to mind when we look at the background from which Joseph negotiated this vow, considering the fact that he made this vow at the tail end of his impactful life as Prime Minister of Egypt.

First, why would he ask that his bones be carried from Egypt? It was a land where he saw many manifestations of God's glory in his life. It was a land that was the bread basket for him and his entire family during the years of famine, and it was a land that had provided him a wife who bore him two great sons, Manasseh and Ephraim. Above all, it was a land where he and his brothers were held in high esteem by Pharaoh and his subjects. After all, his father and forefathers were all buried in the lands where they saw manifestations of the glory of God in their lives.

I believe that Joseph could have made this vow purely based on his faith in the word of God, and also to preserve the mysteries behind his success for future generations of believers who comprise the body of Christ. Like Daniel, we know that Joseph was studious and knowledgeable and therefore knew what God had said to his great grandfather Abraham,

> "... *Know certainly that your descendants will be strangers in a land that is not theirs, and will serve them, and they will afflict them four hundred years. And also the nation whom they serve I will judge; afterward they shall come out with great possessions. Now as for you,*

> *you shall go to your fathers in peace; you shall be buried at a good old age.*
>
> GENESIS 15:13–15 (NKJV)

Here, Joseph was making a prophetic declaration, that the glorious times he and the rest of his kinsmen experienced in Egypt, together with the remarkable legacy and great respect his leadership brought to the children of Israel, needed to be preserved for the benefit of future generations. Unlike the lives of his brothers which were glossed over (Exodus 1:6). Joseph foresaw a situation where the secrets behind his greatness could die-off with the passing of his generation, as was evidenced during the reign of the new Pharaoh some years later, a Pharaoh who did not know about the legacy of Joseph.

The second question that comes to mind is, why would Joseph be silent about the specific location he wanted his bones to be taken to after his death? After all, his own father Israel, at the time of his death in Egypt requested to be buried with his fathers at the *"Cave of Machpelah"* in Hebron, so why would Joseph not want his bones to be buried in this seemingly great mausoleum of his forefathers?

The obvious answer to this question is that after having walked with God throughout his formative years, enduring hatred and rejection from his brothers, to experiencing the trials he finally overcame in Egypt, one thing that became glaringly clear in his mind was a deep understanding of the mistakes committed by members of his immediate family in their individual walks with God.

Here, I also want to submit that being armed with this knowledge, Joseph did not want to go down in the history of his family's lineage as being associated with these mistakes. He wanted to tell the future generations of believers, of

Christians, that you can reach your God-given destiny faster without compromising.

The fight for a fulfilled destiny is fought on the altar of sacrifice.

Third, why didn't the people who executed Joseph's vow by returning his bones to the promised land not bury them anywhere else along the way, but chose to bury them specifically in Shechem? The Bible states that the children of Israel, upon crossing the Red Sea, went through challenges, but the Lord was always with them and manifested Himself in places such as Kadesh, Barnea, and Paran. Their leader Moses, who had remembered the vow, and had taken Joseph's bones with them when they left Egypt, could have decided on any of these sites as a good burial ground, given the favour that God had shown His people in these places, but rather chose not to, even up until he died.

The book of Joshua states that Moses's successor prepared the ground in a unique way for the children of Israel to execute Joseph's vow,

> *So Joshua made a covenant with the people that day, and made for them a statute and an ordinance in Shechem.*
> JOSHUA 24:25 (NKJV)

Notice that it was only after Joshua established a covenant with God on behalf of the children of Israel that the way was paved for the burial of Joseph's bones. It was not by coincidence that the very spot where Joshua had made the covenant with God happened to be the location where Joseph encountered the *'Certain Man'*, and from where he was led into his destiny in Egypt. This spot was the same location where Joseph's bones were buried (Joshua 24:32). I believe Joseph's tomb makes the statement he wanted to convey to the future generations of believers, that *'the secret of my success story is connected to the location where I accepted the burden of godly responsibility and took it upon my shoulders'*. This is the message that was encrypted in his bones.

I also want to submit that Moses, Joshua, and the children of Israel who finally buried Joseph's bones, must have done so from the prophetic realm, where they were enabled to pick up the encrypted message from Joseph, decoded and given to them through divine inspiration to bury the bones in Shechem. The spirit with which Joseph made his vow before his death was God inspired. People like Moses, Joshua, and others who finally buried Joseph's bones were all full of the spirit of God and could dive into the spirit realm and pick up the revelation embedded in Joseph's thinking when he made that vow, in order to execute it accordingly.

What Joseph is saying to you and me here is that in order to function fully with the spirit of excellence, we need to first establish a foundation where we can have a relationship with God and thereafter welcome godly responsibility or burdens as they come our way.

THE DIFFERENT LIFESTYLES IN PERSPECTIVE

I've reserved this conclusion to highlight how the distinctiveness of the life of Joseph differentiated him from his brothers. To this day his life stands out as the epitome of excellence.

Reuben defiled his father's bed by going to bed with his father's concubine Bilhah (Genesis 35:22). Joseph on the other hand, had a similar opportunity to defile his master Potiphar's bed but restrained himself. The bed of a father is a place of productivity. It is a place reserved for the seed of a father to be planted for harvests. The difference is that Reuben initiated the advance to his father's concubine Bilhah. In the case of Joseph, Mrs Potiphar, who was not a relation, offered herself to Joseph, but he resisted (Genesis 39:12). Simply put, Joseph faced an infinitely more tempting situation than Reuben but prevailed.

Simeon and Levi had an opportunity to welcome Shechem, the prince of the lands God willed to Abraham's descendants in Canaan, but failed the test because of his temper (Genesis 34:1–31). No wonder Jacob had to ask for family cleansing after these unfortunate events before proceeding to Bethel (Genesis 35:2–3). Anger is an expression of selfishness. Joseph had a similar opportunity to be angered by the Egyptians who wrongfully accused him and put him in jail. The difference with Joseph was that he was calm even in jail. He realised that these people, although heathens, were central to his ascension into the reign of the Egyptian empire.

When it comes to the value one places on destiny, Joseph was different from Judah. Both men were confronted with tempting situations that required trading their destinies for temporary lustful desires. In the case of Judah, a demand was specifically made on his signet, cord, and staff which represented the Kingship of Israel, and which he gladly relinquished (Genesis 38:18). A similar demand was made on Joseph (Genesis 39:12) but he fled the scene. Obviously, the favour surrounding Joseph (Genesis 39:6–8), and perhaps the bright future that was ahead of him (Genesis 49:12) were the reasons for this temptation. The difference is that Joseph valued his destiny and fought hard to preserve it whilst Judah willingly gave it up on a silver platter.

CONCLUSION

It is obvious that as believers we have been called by God into glorious destinies. Due to veils that the devil sometimes succeeds in putting on us, however, we often miss the road marker to the faster route to fulfillment of destiny. As a result, we succumb to the temptation to settle for a mediocre life.

I have no doubt that the title of this book caught your attention because you wanted to change certain things in your life. You may have endured perpetual crises and trials that have even caused you to contemplate throwing in the towel. I can shed light on the 'why' found in Hosea 4:66 which says that,

> 'My people are destroyed for lack of knowledge.'
>
> (NKJV)

Now that you are armed with this new revelation of truth concerning godly responsibility and wilderness experiences, however, I want to assure you that you are one step closer to achieving an excellent destiny. The tables are about to turn in your favour. Keep on travailing even in your wilderness seasons in order for your 'Zion to come forth' Isaiah 66:8.

In order to arrive at the destination we aspire to, let's take the next step of putting this revelation into practice through faith in Christ Jesus who revealed these truths to us. This is the only way to keep Satan out of our way.

Here are the key points to keep in mind:

- God created each one of us to have an excellent destiny by virtue of His grace that we receive when we accept Jesus Christ as our Lord and Saviour. However, we need godly responsibility to activate the Spirit of Excellence.
- While grace is a gift obtained by believing in Jesus Christ, godly responsibility is earned at the altar of sacrifice. The trials, tribulations, challenges, and unanswered prayers play a part in building godly character in us. This causes us to become responsible.
- Not all environments contain ideal ground for building godly character. The wilderness environment, however, brings our fleshly desires under scrutiny. Here is the ideal place to encounter God.
- When we submit to the purging of our fleshly desires in the wilderness, our spiritual alertness is heightened and this gives us dominion over veils.
- The Spirit of Excellence enables us to leave enduring imprints for future generations.

It is my hope and prayer that having read this book, the good God will grant you the grace to walk in the revelations embedded in these truths as you embark on this journey armed with traits of godly responsibility, dynamically fulfilling divine destiny. Amen!

ABOUT THE AUTHOR

Apostle Richard Owusu Amoaye is a prophet by calling with a mandate to raise champions through God's power for kingdom advancement. He believes that trapped within every person is the seed of greatness and he is on a mission to help people discover and nurture their God given potential so that they can lead purpose driven and impactful lives. Apostle Richard is the visionary and founder of God's Power Ministries (GPM). It is a dynamic apostolic and prophetic ministry which he pioneered in 2010 with his wife Reverend Patrice Amoaye. The diverse and vibrant multi-site ministry is headquartered in Sydney Australia.

The mandate to raise champions, through God's power for kingdom advancement propels Apostle Richard to serve and empower people from all walks of life in a variety of ways including preaching, teaching, mentoring and writing. He is the author of *Decoding the Mystery of Excellence, Power for Exploits* and *The Excellence of Wisdom*. He also wrote the song 'Not Perfect' which is featured on the Greater Grace Power Worship Album. He shares messages of hope and empowerment through a dedicated community magazine called the Prophetic Voice. Not only is he an inspired writer, but he is an astute prophetic preacher and minister of the word at GPM and Richard Amoaye Ministries. He also teaches at the Richard Amoaye Prophetic School which is dedicated to empowering and equipping people who are seeking truth and an understanding of the prophetic gift and ministry.

Apostle Richard came to the saving grace of Christ in his late teenage years and his encounter led him to Power Chapel Worldwide where he was taught and mentored by his father in the Lord Prophet Victor Kusi Boateng. Subsequently, within a relatively short period of time during his service, Apostle Richard received the call into ministry. He worked as an itinerant minister for over a decade. He served in Africa, Europe, North America, and Australasia through prophetic crusades, leadership seminars and church revivals before being called to Sydney Australia. Apostle Richard's love for God knows no bounds and it is what continues to motivate him to share the gospel and offer counsel to many including leaders in Christendom and beyond.

BOOKS BY RICHARD AMOAYE

Power for Exploits

The Excellence of Wisdom

My Secret Place:
Inspired thoughts and Scriptures for daily living
Volumes 1, 2 and 3

Unveiling the heart of prayer

Joy comes in the Morning:
31 days of living in the fullness of Joy in all Circumstances
(Devotional)

To Contact the Author:
Email: info@richardamoayeministries.com
Visit: www.amoaye.org